The
HEART
of
ATTENTION

Free Yourself of Stress, Anxiety,
and All Inner Conflict for Good,
Creating a Heart-felt Life of Perfection

DARLA LUZ

Cover design by Lance Buckley

Although the author has made every effort to ensure that the information in this book was correct at press time, the author and publisher do not assume and hereby disclaim any liability to any party for any loss, damage, or disruption caused by errors or omissions, whether such errors or omissions result from negligence, accident, or any other cause.

The resources in this book are provided for informational purposes only and should not be used to replace the specialized training and professional judgment of a health care or mental health care professional. Neither the author nor the publisher can be held responsible for the use of the information provided within this book. Please always consult a trained professional before making any decision regarding treatment of yourself or others.

The Heart of Attention: Release stress, anxiety, anger, all inner conflict for good and live a life of heart-felt perfection—1st edition

ISBN: 978-1-7348913-0-0

DEDICATION

This book is dedicated to you who will be helped within these pages.

This book is also dedicated to my father,
who lives on in the pages of this book, and who came to me in
spirit to tell me that, "This book is going to help a lot of people."

READ THIS FIRST

DOWNLOAD YOUR FREE WORKBOOK NOW

To get the most out of The Heart of Attention,
as a gift to you, I encourage you to download
a free workbook to use alongside this book.

THE HEART OF ATTENTION WORKBOOK

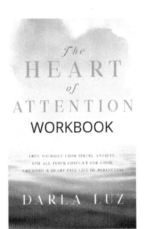

It is important to be active and engaged in any journey.
This workbook will help you to engage by writing down
important turning points, reflections, and progress.

Go to
https://Darlaluzbooks.com/hoaworkbook
To download your free workbook today

TABLE OF CONTENTS

INTRODUCTION

Have you ever felt anxious, stressed, worried, fearful, angry, or any emotional pain or conflict? Your answer might be, "That's life!" I once thought , just as you might, that having anxiety, stress, and any turmoil was a normal part of life.

But is it really? For sure it is not living life to its maximum joyous and peaceful fulfillment that each of us craves.

No one should feel anxious, stressed, sad, or isolated. Each of us have an inborne right to feel maximum joyous and peaceful fulfillment in life.

You might be wondering how I can make such a statement. I once had overwhelming thoughts and emotions that circled endlessly blocking my own enthusiasm for life. Today, I live free of anxiety and stress, as well as all inner conflict.

However, there *are* moments when I am challenged by the daily bombardment of bad news that confronts all of us, or I may be challenged by something that did not turn out the way I expected. But *only for a moment*, because I use the same practices and tools that I am giving you here to live in heart-felt perfection, directing my life, and not allowing out-of-control thoughts and emotions to enslave and imprison me.

You will discover in between these pages that, in an instant, you too can feel light-hearted and have clarity of mind, dissolving the lesser energies that weigh you down and depress you.

The tools in this book are the first step to living consciously aware and free of all inner turmoil that will give you a better life of less struggle and more ease and help you get there in a much faster way than I did.

DISSOLVING INNER
CONFLICT FOR GOOD

It may be hard to believe, but you *can* release *for good* any thought, emotion, feeling, belief, and memory that does not make you feel good! You will discover that a simple shift from where you now hold your attention will help you to let go of all that weighs you down and depresses you. Through the doorway of your breath, you will find inner peace, calm, and relaxation, and this is the first step to healing from the difficulties of life.

Whatever we put attention on grows and creates our experience. When we feel drained and exhausted, zapped of our vitality, our very energy for life, we are most likely giving attention to intense thoughts that circle endlessly, giving fuel to intense emotions. The attention we give to unwanted thoughts and emotions puts stress on our psyche and physical body, producing endless emotional pain and anguish, which may potentially cause us great harm, affecting every aspect of our life.

When we experience any kind of loss, whether a loss of a job, a relationship, or a loved one, we feel disheartened and devastated. There may be a deep hole within, filled with loneliness and isolation, making us feel separate from everything and everyone. We may fall prey to endless thoughts and emotions that circle and loop, making us feel stuck and trapped in sadness and despair. Many people experience life as a constant barrage of daily disruptions and irritations that cause an ongoing, low-grade, almost imperceptible feeling of anxiety.

 Even if you feel anxiety and stress only occasionally, you've come to the right place.

You will begin the process of letting go of thoughts, feelings, and emotions that sadden, weaken, and depress you at the same moment you do the first practice in this book. You will be in a safe place of no conflict in which unwanted thoughts and emotions cannot enter.

My hope is that in telling my own challenging experience, which was the catalyst that lead to the writing of this book, you will become aware and understand, as I have, that life can be lived simply, yet powerfully, within the meaningful joy and aliveness of our heart. For to experience the expansive boundlessness of our heart, through the doorway of our calm and relaxed breath, is to find a safe haven, free of inner conflict and pain.

MY STORY

My challenge was one of those situations in life that makes us feel as if our world is ending.

From the beginning of our marriage, my husband and I bought into a societal belief that accumulating properties, cars, and gadgets would bring "happiness" at some point in the future. As a result, we set out to build wealth. We could not have foreseen a devastating job loss through the disruption of a new technology. We did not anticipate an economic downturn that demolished our assets like a delicate sandcastle taken back by the sea.

On the verge of losing our home, thoughts and emotions circled over and over again as I stayed awake in the eerie silence of the night, ruminating about past mistakes and worrying about a dreadful future. Could we ever recover our loss? What would the future hold for our children? In the dark abyss that I had initiated within, I could not envision a bright future. In darkness, I needed light.

INTRODUCTION

Little did I know that I would find a bright future in the bright sunlight of a natural landscape

The symbolic nature of light runs through this book like the threads of a tapestry. For we are nourished and soothed with sunlight and healed within with light.

DARKNESS CANNOT SURVIVE THE LIGHT

I began a daily drive to the comforting light of a beautiful lake surrounded by rolling hills, embraced by a ten-thousand-foot snow-capped mountain. As weeks turned into months, I continued my twenty-to thirty-minute appointment simply contemplating the calming, even flows of the water; the birds' easy glide on flowing air currents; the glistening mountain peak that loomed against a sky the color of the lake. I observed the scene before me in a depth of awareness I had never known. The most insignificant object turned significant in those rich moments as I watched, with fascination, the rhythmic tempo of a single blade of grass!

The chatterbox of doom and gloom, which I once could not turn off, simply stopped in those moments. I had nothing to obsess or worry about. Most importantly, I had no problems. They had simply vanished and dissolved through my *lack of attention on them*!

A simple shift from where you now hold your attention will help you to let go of all that weighs you down and depresses you.

In a calm and relaxed way, you will practice in this book to let go of all inner turmoil. As if that weren't reward enough, because of your now clear, pure, spaciousness within,--free of anxiety, stress, and all conflict—you will get inspirational ideas and insights about the next steps you should take to move your life forward to a higher, better future. These are the gifts and rewards that make life seem magical and effortless.

AN INSPIRATIONAL IDEA

One day as I started my car, I got a strong impulse to drive to a point on the other side of the lake. I knew exactly when to turn and when to go straight. It felt as if a driving force was pulling me toward a destination, even though I was very aware and alert. I knew to stop at the end of a cul-de-sac in front of a vacant house with a view of the lake and a for-sale sign on the front lawn. And an inspirational idea came to me. Why not call the real estate agent listed on the sign and ask if I could move my family in and stage the house with our furniture until it sold?

In an effortless way, I found a company that staged homes, allowing a family to live in them. For the next four years, my husband, my two children, and I lived in ready-to-be-shown, staged homes! I began doing something I loved, and my family learned organizational skills. What could have been a painful transition to move from a home we lost turned into excitement once we moved into a home we could care for.

My inspirational idea, that seemed to magically appear, turned out perfectly. Once my tension, worry, anxiety, all emotionally-draining feelings fell away, my silent, peaceful, calm within created the spaces so that I could receive a clear inspirational idea. It made perfect sense to use what was left of our financial devastation, our furniture, to solve our problem.

Do we make life more difficult than it needs to be. What was this life force that made itself known once my inner turmoil fell away, that seemed so loving and gentle, nudging and prodding me on so I could find my way in the clarity of the moment?

Is it intuition, which is a "knowing" beyond our rational mind, a Universal One Mind to which each of us is connected, or is it a Universal life force energy that makes itself known when we kneel in prayer and open ourselves in sincere, heartfelt truth expressing our most profound yearnings and aspirations? You would probably agree that it is a Higher Power. Most of us have asked for a helping hand when we've felt overwhelmed. You might call it God, The Universe, Creation, The True Self, or Presence. Which ever way you perceive it is fine.

As you breathe deeply and feel inner peace in the practices here, feel free to incorporate whatever belief you may have of a Higher Power, or you may simply feel the freedom inner peace provides. Eitherl way, you will discover through a cumulative effect that you can let go for good of all that hinders and blocks you from a better life.

The ensuing years after my experience at the lake brought more ecomomic ups and downs, and unfortunately, I had not yet learned the tools I share with you here that could have saved me years of inner turmoil that continued to plague me. I did, however, go within in peaceful meditation, which seemed to help the situations in my life unfold in a smoother way.

But it wasn't until I began a spiritual awakening path in 2011 that aligned my energy centers—known as chakras in yoga—that my life, in general, took a higher path. To "align" the energy centers simply means to be in harmony and balance with the flow of life.

The practices you will do here is a beginning to help you balance and harmonize your life through feelings that are calm and peaceful.

As I began my spiritual path, I had vivid dreams night after night of hundreds of pages that downloaded before me. I didn't understand what was written on these pages because they downloaded very rapidly. One night in my dream I made an effort to get close enough in alert awareness and read the word "thoughts." On another morning, I hurriedly sketched a book cover that I saw clearly in a dream. It was clear to me that I was being shown a book I was going to write. Who was I to write a book about "thoughts?" I had problems with overwhelming thoughts in my own life! My spiritual path helped open me to my life purpose and to writing this book. I always wanted to write a helpful book. I had no idea how or what I would write about. As it turned out, my more spacious mind, now opened to inspirational ideas and insightst, helped to materialize this book.

Researching and writing turned out to be therapeutic as I studied the philosophies and traditions thousands of years old and the lectures and writings of modern-day spiritual teachers. I found that we are much more powerful than we believe. Once we choose where we put our attention, we can change our life! We are, at our core, *a Being of awareness and light.* Living in the awareness of ourselves as a high energetic light will now provide our life with harmonious and balanced situations that seem miraculous!

Little did I know that as I began writing this book, I was about to receive the reward of a "will" that is different from "will power." I was provided with a will that gave me the enthusiasm and eagerness to write and finish this book! Each and everyone of us are gifted and rewarded in ways that fulfill who we are when we let go of what no longer serves our life—the mind of lesser energy thoughts and emotions that obstructs our path to a better life.

MY STORY CONTINUES...
A SURPRISE "GIFT."

A couple of years after beginning my spiritual path and after yet another economic downturn we had managed to save enough to purchase another home.

Our real estate agent sent us the first group of listings of homes for sale. The next day, he called to tell us he had called the agent representing the house we had "check marked." I told him we had not check marked any house. He said that was strange because there was a check-marked house that was bank-owned and had a lake view from almost every room, and it had to be seen in person because the picture did not do it justice.

The following day, we walked into a house at the end of a cul-de-sac with a 180-degree view of a lake from almost every room.. Amazingly, this view of the center of the lake was very similar to the lake view I had looked out on and found comfort in so many years before. We were lead to this house that had been "check marked" for us, that sat on a bluff at the end of a cul-de-sac, overlooking a lake. Even still, I did not realize the full connection of the mysterious similarities that unfolded until we moved in. This house we now lived in was an hour's drive from the house at the end of a cul-de-sac with a lake view that I had been "pulled" toward many years earlier. A house that had inspired an idea to help me solve a problematic situation! The connections that once proved to be incredibly magical and mysterious were, almost two decades later, still fitting together perfectly!

The gifts and rewards continued in helpful ways as I wrote this book A random page in a book or a conversation gave me ideas and information, even before I needed the information! The same dollar amount spent on a more comfortable chair for my writing desk mysteriously re-appeared. An amazing and very mystifying "help" happened one morning. Just before falling asleep one night, I asked about this book. The answer came in the morning as I shopped, stepped away to retrieve a few items, and came back to find a book, which looked as if it had been "tossed" into my shopping cart from a nearby bookshelf, with the exact answer to my question! I no longer question the "magic." My growing conscious-aware spiritual path reflects back into my life calm inner peace and trust; a life that works for me, and not against me.

WHAT YOU WILL GET OUT OF THIS BOOK

We are part of an amazing and meticulously orchestrated universe that created our equally amazing mental, emotional, and physical Self. We are made of the same elements. We are stardust. Knowing how to connect with it is imperative.

Through the practices in this book that take you to a light-filled infinite energy field, you will learn how to connect with the universe and these elements. As you practice in the light, effortlessly aware of your breath and inner Self, you will, without doubt, let go of the darkness of difficulties and discord. Darkness cannot survive in light. We see it every morning at sunrise. But it will take practice. The same kind of practice we all did as a baby learning to walk and talk.

In chapter three, you will be helped to be more positive, and gain insight about how your brain will actually help you in your quest to live in the higher energies of appreciation and affirmed positive statements, allowing you to more easily let go of lesser energies that are the cause of hardship and suffering.

My hope is that within these pages, you will gain a new calmness and have a more accepting nature, and yet be more powerful than ever because you will now live in awareness, simply observing life's drama and not becoming involved in it. You will be reminded of what you already know but often forget—the beauty that truly exists in the world-- because of our daily exposure, immersion, and involvement in "bad news."

Having inner peace will make life easier as circumstances and situations in your life change for the better because we live in a mirror-projected universe that reflects back whatever we think and feel.

The proof that your life is moving forward in a better direction will come as you realize that your life is freer of difficulties and problems because you now turn away quickly from the problem-infused darkness and choose light.

My hope for you is that you will practice here and continue a lifetime path of Consciousness that reflects back to you the same energy of limitless possibilities. As incredible as it may sound, you, as an important part of the human collective, will now help a world in jeopardy simply by injecting your positive inner peace, overpowering the stronghold of negative energies.

The more you practice, the more you will live in the higher energy of light, which is the most important thing you can do in your life!

DO IT AS IF YOUR LIFE DEPENDS ON IT, BECAUSE IT DOES!

The last practice in this book will help you to let go *for good* of all low energies that sadden and depress. Through a cumulative effect of doing the practice, taking only seconds, you will understand and realize without effort or hard work that all lower energies that do not make you feel good have no significance, no meaning, and no power. This alone will change your life! The attention you give to the practices within these pages that feel most comfortable to you will lead to an experience of a life of more ease, joy, fulfillment, and peace!

THE MYSTERIOUS
AND BEAUTIFUL FORCES

I never cease being appreciative of what the "gift" of the lake view offers every day. One evening recently, the sky in the west turned crimson and a brilliant white moon peeked, then fully emerged like a luminous sphere of light, a beacon floating against an eastern cobalt sky, reflecting on the water, finding full light and blossoming in ultimate fulfillment on the earth plane. A glittery silvery streak containing dazzling, dancing white light, became a mirror in darkening water, revealing the shadowy figures of tiny passing ducks.

I have come to understand that to live life engaged in sounds, sights, scents, tastes, touch, and *feeling* is to turn the ordinary into delightful, the mundane into joy. The vast space within each of us, now emptied and freed, knows only the good feelings of optimism, joy, delight, love, and compassion.. The more we *feel the higher energies, the better we connect, and the better life becomes.*

I hope the words I have written here convey the heartfelt depth and ease of flow that came from beyond my physical mind. The mind beyond our physical mind is connected to the mysteriously beautiful force that aligns in the spirit of "helping others." It lines up with thoughts, like my own thoughts of writing and materializing this book.

INTRODUCTION

It is a Beautiful Force that plots, plans, and designs toward the highest good for all concerned. This power emerges in a spectrum of possibilities, finding full light on the earth plane, and blossoming into its ultimate fulfillment. You, as the reader, are part of this fulfillment.

Let's begin your path to a better life, one that you no longer look back on with grief and regret...because it is your birthright and your deserve it!

Chapter One

THE HEART OF CONSCIOUSNESS

CONSCIOUSNESS IS AN ANCIENT GIFT HUMANITY MUST OPEN *NOW*

Ancient texts have, for thousands of years, written about the power within each of us. We, humans, have had the inborn tools to live in harmony and bliss, with far less struggle and more ease, since we first set foot on Earth. We have simply lost our way, gotten trapped and stuck in a world that does not yet realize the grave danger of focused attention in the low energies of division and discord.

THE URGENCY OF CONSCIOUSNESS
IN TODAY'S WORLD

It is urgent to find our True Self in Consciousness. As we do, everything can change, including our world. Humanity's increasing light and virtuous qualities can then easily blanket the darkness in the world—as easily as the sunrise blankets the darkness with morning light.

When we let go of inner conflict and live with the attention and awareness of our Self within, we create the freed-up space for our virtuous qualities to seep to the surface. Imagine a world in which humanity opened to Consciousness and let go of all outer conflict. The virtuous qualities of love and compassion, inner peace, joy, and a new connectedness would arise. The unconsciousness of all conflict we experience in the world today—war, divisiveness, greed, selfishness, all darkness—would fall away. We cannot fight this darkness without getting involved in it ourselves through frustration, anger, and disappointment. We have to *find* the light within.

Over millennia, masters, monks, and sages practiced aware attention on the inner life force energies, the breath, and the stream of life within. Sometimes they focused attention on a flickering candle or the smallest light-filled hole, enclosing themselves in darkness. In calm peace, they brought a wandering mind back, again and again, to a focused attention within. Whatever method was used to shift the mind from unfocused wandering to attention on the life force energy within, they experienced the rewards that came from hours of daily practice. They celebrated the peace, joy, love, and compassion that resulted from the freed-up space of a mind that once experienced confusion and turmoil. The revealed and unveiled True Self of harmony, balance, joy, and love lead to the first spiritual paths.

In the time of Buddha, twenty-six hundred years ago, keen insight into the mind developed into a "science of the mind" and an "experiential knowing." In essence, Buddha told his followers to follow him only if they experienced what he had experienced. Followers were instructed to put aware attention only on each chore as they were doing it in the moment, thereby releasing anxious, painful thoughts and misery, healing the suffering of the masses. As many became free of the emotional pain, anxiety, and despair, "enlightenment" became the new pursued way of being. An experience of freedom from emotional pain now brought about a natural arising of joy, peace, and compassion. A new path was lit, which Buddha called "the end of suffering."

Six hundred years later, Jesus walked among his followers, praising and radiating love, the highest energy in the universe, healing the masses through a pure, virtuous quality. He spoke of "salvation," of being rescued, always embodying and exemplifying the virtuous quality of love.

Both Jesus and Buddha spoke of being relieved and rescued, of ending suffering and gaining freedom. But relieved, rescued, and gaining freedom from what?

We were encouraged through its mystery to find our own answers.

What is it that makes us suffer and keeps us imprisoned and enslaved so we don't feel free?

The answer is our mind.

In 1890, an American psychologist, author, and philosopher, William James, who today is remembered as the father of psychology, uncovered an important psychological function of the mind that is key to a better life. He wrote that "voluntarily bringing back a wandering attention, over and over again, is the very root of judgment, character, and will." And, as if looking into the future, "without selective interest (*attention*), experience is an utter chaos."

However, as we, the human collective, release the wandering attention we put on negativity, giving aware *attention* to a more pure and simple life force within, we become more clear, alert, and wise. Freed of wandering thinking, new insight becomes available to heal not only our own life but our planet as well because we share its elements and minerals.

Gandhi was right. We must *be* the change we want to see in the world.

Something magical happens once we become the change we want to see in the world. The high-vibrational energy of Consciousness can go out to others and spread as in reverberation and resonance because light is many more times stronger than darkness. We can now change the world by our mere presence.

Consciousness is an evolutionary life force affecting each of us, as well as all life forms on our planet and beyond. Each of us can tap into this great power. The high vibrational energies coming in through our solar system can help us tap into this powerful life force energy. Each year, these energies will become more intense. It is crucial to live in the higher energies, consciously aware and free of inner conflict, because how we feel will reflect back in our lives as situations and circumstances. You will practice here to live in the higher energies of inner peace, joy, and aliveness.

You will be encouraged again and again throughout this book to practice being consciously aware of yourself and your surroundings. *You are Consciousness and you are awareness.* Being consciously aware of yourself and your surroundings will lead you to who you really are—your True Self, your innermost and truest nature.

As your consciously aware True Self, you become free of anguish, you become open, uplifted, and optimistic, able to see life's beauty and more able than ever to see what really matters. It is as if you are rewarded. That is when the powerful life force energies attract "magic" into your life through situations and events that effortlessly fall into place! Life becomes easier, with less struggle.

In a world that insists on bad news, there cannot be better news than this!

THE HEART OF CONSCIOUSNESS

1. Humanity has had inborn tools to live in balance, harmony, and bliss, with far less struggle and more ease since we first set foot on Earth. We have lost our way because we have focused and put attention in the low energies of anger, anxiety, stress, and discord.

2. Attention and awareness of ourselves within will heal not only ourselves but our planet as well because we are so connected to it, sharing its elements.

3. When we release the wandering attention we put on the low energy of inner conflict, we free up space for the higher energies of love and compassion, peace, and joy.

4. The higher energies then attract "magic and miracles" into our life.

Chapter Two

WHAT IS CONSCIOUSNESS?

*Consciousness is as simple as looking into the face
of a flower and realizing a shared connection.
We too open to the light in strength and beauty*

Millions upon millions of words have been written in an effort to describe Consciousness. Yet, it remains a mystery. It is as incomprehensible as the infinite night sky, which, it now seems, contains an infinity of stars and planets. We seem to have an intuitive knowing that we connect to something beyond measure, something that renders us speechless. We are stirred as we watch a lunar or solar eclipse. We are awestruck by the visual beauty of a rainbow. We take in, mesmerized, the shimmering moonbeams on water. And we may finally realize, as we ponder the face of a flower, that we, too, open to the light and grow in strength and beauty.

Words like incomprehensible and indestructible have been used to define Consciousness and can define who we are as well, for when we become our Selves in Consciousness, we awaken to its eternal connection, linked to an immense and vast space. The *feeling* of this immense and vast space when we are in the purity of our essence, our heart, translates into infinite possibilities in our life. There are then no limitations to what we can be, have, or do.

There is no reason to feel small in an infinite universe. For each of us carries the limitless space within and all around us in each instant, making us a limitless being that reflects unlimited and infinite potential in our lives.

Despite all the determined attempts and efforts to describe Consciousness, it remains profoundly easy to attain and is accessible, *now*. Connecting to it is as simple as feeling good. With practice, we can ride its upward spiral filled with bliss by landing softly within ourselves.

Consciousness is life itself. It is seeing life all around us with the conscious-aware freshness we had as a child. It is living from the centered heart of our Self, right in the middle, with awareness and focused attention of our breathing self and what surrounds us. It has taken humanity thousands of years to wander far from our "home" of Consciousness.

But we can get it back in this instant. There is no waiting involved. Today, each one of us may find the doorway to Consciousness in an easier way than ever.

Ultra-high rays of energy are making their way through our solar system in a more powerful way than ever. Each and every one of us is a part of this alive energy that is mystifying and abundant. We share its elements and can match and align with it when we shift our attention to our breath in calming peace.

The journey to save ourselves and to end suffering begins by shifting our attention to a better place. Each and every one of us can end our suffering. We can all be saved from the detrimental effect of a mind we cannot control.

WHERE IS YOUR ATTENTION NOW?

Are you immersed in "problems," allowing the mind of unwanted thoughts to circle again and again, with no solution? Are you reliving what someone said last week, a month ago, years ago, or a lifetime ago? Are you worrying about something that might happen? Or maybe you're thinking that if only someone was different, you would not have this "problem."

SHIFT ATTENTION TO "THE HEART OF YOURSELF" THROUGH THE DOORWAY OF THE BREATH

Are you feeling "down" at this moment? Your breath can calm you and create peace within. Once your attention is on your life-giving breath and on your life force energy within, it is as if the door closes on unwanted thoughts, emotions, feelings, memories, self-doubts—whatever bothers you and makes you feel "down." You are protected, safe, and at peace as you shift attention to the life force within you, which can be accessed as quickly as this moment. Living life in the pure and natural state of conscious awareness of your Self, without unwanted thoughts, is what will soothe, calm, and help you to release harmful and detrimental thoughts that come from an unconscious mind.

When our mind wanders uncontrolled, we suffer. As we shift a wandering mind to give attention to our Self within and life surrounding us at this moment, we relieve suffering. We are in a place that is safe and secure, a safe haven, a shelter. To live *from this space* is powerful.

Once the mind is quieted and stilled, we are free to *feel* life's goodness. Increasingly, the virtuous qualities of love, compassion, peace, and joy will naturally arise. We need not work hard to try and acquire these virtuous qualities. They become evident as we remove the fear-driven, weighed-down mind. Our innermost being, our True Self, who we really are, now comes to the surface.

Notice and be conscious of what you may be attracting into your life. It is vital to understand and become aware of a universal "law" that attracts into your life whatever you think, say, or do. Thoughts are energy and attract into your life whatever you are thinking—good or bad. If your thoughts are in the past or in the future, you most likely are indulged and immersed in the mind of unwanted thoughts and emotions. Unwanted thoughts and emotions can attract unwanted situations and circumstances into your life. You may be remembering a *time* in the past that did not end well, or you may be worrying about a *time* that *may* transpire. Become aware of lower-energy thoughts so you can shift your attention to a better place, a *timeless* present moment.

Consciousness is in the middle heart of yourself. The ancient school of wisdom emphasized our core, our innermost self, in relation to Consciousness. This ancient wisdom called attention to what was good and powerful within us. Our personality, everyday self, looms big in our lives today. The personality becomes distracted and unfocused through an experience of what happens to us daily.

Sadly, we get lost as we become immersed and involved in what happened in the past or what may happen in the future. We are living life in a measurement of time rather than the dimension of a timeless place of our inner Self. You are protected and safe in a timeless place where there is nothing to obsess or worry about. *Feel* the safety, protection, and the freedom as you let go in the following practice.

Practice: Dissolving unwanted thoughts

Do the following practice when you feel burdened and overwhelmed by an unconscious, fear-driven, or angry mind:

In full awareness of your breath, take two or three deep breaths to become calm. Continue inhaling and exhaling in an even, comfortable flow. While maintaining an awareness of your breath, add awareness of life streaming through your inner Self—life flowing through your heart, your bloodstream, and your cells, from your head to your toes. Add awareness of your surroundings, still maintaining awareness of your breath and inner Self. Stay positive and relaxed. If your mind wanders, bring it back to awareness of all three at once—your breath, inner Self, and surroundings.

You will feel calmer and lighter, no longer weighed down with burdens and problems. Even a few seconds of aware attention on your breath, inner Self, and surroundings are helpful. The time you spend, from a few seconds to five or ten minutes at a time, has a cumulative effect, making it easier and easier to shift the wandering mind to the peace and calm of your Self within. Practice staying in alert awareness of your Self and your surroundings.

Going into the rich space of quiet peace and calm, leaving behind the chaos of a frenzied world, does much more than you might think. The more time you spend here, the more you will notice situations unfold in a smoother way as you go about your daily activities. At that moment, you are helping your physical body to find ease rather than "dis-ease." You are also protecting your mental and emotional health. You will feel lighter, less weighed down, and more able to face situations as they unfold during your day. And, as you will learn in the next chapter, you are helping your brain's ability to restructure itself, increasing its ability to be positive and more alert and aware.

Notice that as you become aware of the life force energy of your Self within, unwanted thoughts cannot enter. This is the beginning of freedom, the beginning of feeling safe and secure. Most importantly, it is the beginning of feeling a more powerful you.

Life was not meant to be filled with the emotional pain of anger, fear, and difficulties! You came into this world through an awareness of your breath, your inner being, and your sense perceptions. Come back to the clean slate that was you as you came into this physical existence.

You can remove negativity in the same moment you decide to release it. Remember to relax and take a deep breath when you *feel* down. Bring yourself back to the calm feeling of your breath, in aware attention of "the heart of yourself." Little by little, you will gain the power to be at the helm of your life, no longer enslaved by an out-of-control mind. You will be in calm peace with focused attention on your life force energy within. This is how you will not only free yourself from experiencing the "problems" and the "difficulties" of life but also how you will prevent damage and harm to your mental, emotional, and physical self.

It does not mean, of course, that you will never have problems or difficulties again. It means that you will not *feel* them anymore. We live in a challenging and difficult world. It is vital to protect yourself from an outside world's tremendous onslaught of negativity. And your breath is the doorway to do this.

PRACTICES AND SUMMARY
OF CHAPTER TWO

WHAT IS CONSCIOUSNESS?

1. *Practice: Dissolving unwanted thoughts*

   Do the following practice when you feel burdened and
   overwhelmed with unwanted thoughts:

   Take two or three deep breaths, or as many as you need to
   become calm. Inhale and exhale in an even, comfortable
   flow. Maintaining an awareness of your breath, add
   awareness of life streaming through your inner Self—life
   flowing through your heart, your bloodstream, and your
   cells, from your head to your toes. Add awareness of your
   surroundings, while still maintaining awareness of your
   breath and inner Self. Stay positive and relaxed. If your
   mind wanders, bring it back to awareness of all three at
   once—your breath, your inner Self, and your surroundings.

2. Practice seeing life all around you with the conscious-aware
   freshness you had as a child.

3. Connecting to Consciousness is easy and effortless. It is as
   simple as breathing deeply and relaxing in calm awareness
   and acceptance. Look at your surroundings and accept life
   just as it is.

4. Feel the freedom, the lightness, and the safe haven of the timeless space of your inner Self.

5. Become aware of thoughts that take you to past pain or future worry. When our thoughts are in the past or in the future, most likely they are negative, useless, low-energy thoughts.

6. Where are your thoughts now? Be conscious of what you may be attracting into your life, whether good or bad. We attract, as situations, whatever we think, say, or do.

7. Releasing inner conflict does not mean you will never have difficulties or challenges again. However, you will not *feel* them anymore.

SUMMARY

1. We all have within us an immense space without limits and boundaries. When we connect to this vast space, we become open to limitless possibilities in our life.

2. Humanity has strayed far from our home of Consciousness in an experience of conflict and struggle rather than the more effortless experience of ease and harmony. But we can get it back in an instant!

3. When our mind wanders, we suffer. The mind of focused
    attention *now* does not suffer.

Chapter Three

EMPOWERING YOURSELF

*To purposefully see the beauty that
surrounds you is to empower yourself*

A most amazing finding has come from neuroscience,
which is the study of the structure and functionality of the
brain. Through brain imaging, this newer, emerging science
can now unequivocally tell us that our brain can restructure
itself as we become positive. Every moment that a positive
thought enters our mind, we are benefitting our brain—and
our life!

In as short a timeframe as an hour and a half, the brain can
begin a process of restructuring by thickening the left
prefrontal lobe of positivity and making the right prefrontal
lobe of negativity thinner. The brain will change through what
is called plasticity and become malleable and flexible, helping
you to stay more positive in the future. You can begin this

process as you *purposefully* and *deliberately* become more positive, now—at this moment—by seeing the "glass half full, rather than half empty." Why not turn your attention to a life that can be lived more easily in positive enjoyment, rather than a life filled with stress, anxious worry, and emotional pain?

We humans have about sixty thousand thoughts per day. It has been estimated that 80 to 90 percent of thoughts are useless and detrimental to our mental and physical health. Imagine drawing a line on a clean sheet of paper each time a thought comes through. There would be no clarity, no way to see the blank, clear sheet anymore. Is it any wonder that in our daily lives we are filled with confusion and the inability to think clearly?

Our world is divided. We see things as bad or good. We argue our viewpoint over another's viewpoint. We believe things to be black or white, up or down, sad or happy, beginning or ending. Everything seems to be polarized, filled with divisions and discord, never coming together, in conversations, governments, the news of the day, and relationships. Nothing in our outer experience seems to come to the midway point of understanding. In every situation, it seems, somebody wins and another has to lose; no one comes to a centered, more unified point of view.

When you realize that your thoughts are separated and split— either thinking about the painful past or a worrisome future, either liking or disliking, either arguing whether something is left or right, up or down—remember to take cover in the simple and pure space within. As you do, you will leave behind a divided, dualistic, and polarized world. You will also keep a needed distance from fearful and angry thoughts and emotions that insist on delivering low energy.

As you do this, you will not be fighting, trying to get rid of, or battling negativity. Instead, through practice, you will easily and effortlessly find your natural harmony and balance.

SEE THE BIGGER PICTURE

Look over past events of your life. Do you remember more events that you judged as bad? We tend to emphasize and remember mostly the bad events, causing needless pressure on ourselves. However, if instead we look at all that has transpired in our life as one long chain of events, we can see more clearly how we arrived at this point today. Now we can more clearly see how certain events were needed to move us forward in life.

Ever since humans set off on space exploration in the early 1950s, a mysterious event occurred that astronauts experienced in orbit, prompting their own observance that the "real reason" they went to the moon was to see Earth. Upon seeing the beautiful, blue sphere of their planet home from afar, they pondered on our human existence. As they did, they saw the bigger picture, the truth of our human history, the emerging consequences of our choices. Feeling emotionally stirred, they decided to help make things better by starting organizations, writing, and talking about their experience of "awakening" so far from home.

By seeing the bigger picture of our lives and standing back objectively, we see, not so much the negativity, but the truth, stirring the depths of our virtuous qualities, which can then become a positive turning point. From a different perspective and vantage point, everything can be seen that brought us to this point, a point of more wisdom and growth. For some, it may be a little scary to look back, but if it's done with the intention of looking at the good that came out of situations, eventually the negatives won't loom so large. The more we ponder our own life from a distance, the more we see only the truth of what has transpired, and from there, we gain a desire to evolve and grow.

We must put a positive spin on past events rather than circling thoughts of "poor me" as the victim. Looking upon your past as a positive experience allows you to move forward into a more accepting, more joyous experience of future events. When others go over their problems, you might help them view their problems in a more positive way. As you look back on your own life as "bad" experiences, you can now see how what you looked upon as "bad" was needed so other "good" could be experienced. Now you can see how the job you lost that was so disturbing allowed for a better, more enjoyable job today. Now you can see how the breakup that devastated you allowed you to meet someone better suited. Now you understand how the horrendous loss of your home and belongings led to an understanding of what is really important in life.

As you look back on your life and gain the bigger, clearer picture, you also gain a new optimism that life's situations can be helpful rather than just "bad." You grow in awareness that emotional pain comes not from another person or event, but from the way you have interpreted an event as "bad." Seeing the big picture of past events in a more positive light helps you become insulated to a good degree, shielded from an outside chaotic world. As you become aware of how "bad" can turn into "good," it becomes easier to open to the possibility of a future that leads to more joy and fulfillment.

Neuroscientist Dr. Richard Davidson says today's brain imaging technology can see the effects on the brain when one releases the lower energy of negative thoughts and emotions to become more positive. It is as if the brain rebuilds and a whole new architecture emerges, opening to new, more positive experiences because of your new outlook on life. The outcome of your relationships, your career, every area of life can transform for the better as you become more positive.

By developing the skill of being positive, you add to your brain's transformative abilities that, in turn, can transform you. You have much to gain by being positive as you change a negative reaction into a positive thought. And changing from negative to positive quickly, at the same moment you become aware of a moody and weighed-down feeling, can become a positive, new skill.

Once you are more positive, unwanted thoughts become more visible, more obvious. Acquiring a habit of noticing negativity coming into your space at this moment is the beginning of freedom! (You will learn more about simply observing a thought in later chapters.) As you observe a negative thought, you become detached and are outside of the negativity, no longer wallowing in it. Because you are simply noticing it and not indulging in the thought, it loses power.

You are creating mind strength as you become more positive. Just as we exercise our physical body, we can also benefit from mental exercises, helping our minds to develop ease, calm, and strength, improving our mental health. Practicing mind exercises is as easy as calming the physical body through your breath. Once the physical body is calmed, the mind follows.

Most importantly, you are now directing your life, guiding it in the direction you want. You are no longer in the grip of a relentlessly negative mind that has an addictive characteristic, holding you hostage. You are the one in charge!

THE SLOW BUT SURE
DISMANTLING OF NEGATIVITY

When we give undivided, focused attention on the unwanted thoughts that produce pessimism, bad moods, and a general demoralizing attitude, we suffer. Focused attention on unwanted thoughts also destroys health, impairs relationships, and can lead to a shorter lifespan. This is only the beginning, the tip of the iceberg, of a long list of forces that influence our lives negatively! Imagine the many different ways people all over the world internalize lower energies every day. Imagine, too, how our planet is being destroyed by lower-energy thoughts coming from divisive, greedy entities. Thoughts are energies, and they permeate throughout our environment. This lower energy—stemming from thoughts of fear, anger, hatred, and divisiveness—infiltrating environments all over the world further adds to the depressed state of a planet with which we are so connected.

Fortunately, the higher energies of Consciousness, which are increasingly awakening the human collective, are many more times stronger than weaker, lower energies. We, each of us, can help to awaken those around us by radiating the higher energies of cooperation, compassion, peace, joy, and kindness, which arise naturally as we expand our Consciousness.

Roald Dahl said, "Watch with glistening eyes the whole world around you because the greatest secrets are always hidden in the most unlikely places."

Begin now to make each moment the best. As you look at your surroundings, look only for the best—the best intentions and actions of others, the good that will come from whatever you experience, even a positive experience with the weather. The rain will bring nourishment and growth to the trees, the foliage, the flowers, and to the tiniest of creatures. As you do errands, look around at things you have never really noticed. The beautiful architecture of the library, the school, the post office, the city hall, and people's smiles as they greet each other, the way the sunlight highlights the trees as you walk down a city sidewalk. By keeping your mind fully anchored and busy on only the positive, you will not be met with resistance or unwanted thoughts trying to come into your space. When you are busy putting attention on only the positive, negativity simply disappears, losing its stronghold over you. Cultivate an ongoing atmosphere of being positive.

Allowing negativity to infiltrate your mind for even a few seconds will make you want to get rid of it or try to push away unwanted, negative thoughts, emotions, and feelings, increasing their resistance so they then persist. This is why negative thoughts and emotions circle endlessly, and it becomes difficult to stop them.

Ancient texts have, for thousands of years, encouraged a non-judgmental and peaceful way to dissolve thoughts. Being non-judgmental of a thought is important because once you judge and battle with a thought, you revert back to the small, false mind, which is known as "the ego" (you will learn about the ego in later chapters). The small, false mind is critical and very judgmental.

One way to lessen the attention and importance we put on negative thoughts is to say the word "thinking" when we notice an unwanted thought. When we simply acknowledge an unwanted thought, without getting involved in its content, we weaken its strength. Let's say you are driving and suddenly you become aware of an unwanted, negative thought. As you say "thinking" and give full aware attention on driving, your lack of attention to the content of the thought will easily dissolve it. Simply acknowledging an unwanted thought passing through by saying "thinking" is used in meditation in the East and can also be used as you practice becoming positive daily.

POSITIVE STATEMENTS
CAN TURN YOUR LIFE AROUND

Sometimes we give thoughts a stronghold by allowing them to circle repeatedly as we hear past voices of negative comments about ourselves. We may hear these voices from long ago of siblings, parents, teachers, or bosses. "You never do anything right!" "You'll never amount to anything!"

Anything that we hold onto and believe about ourselves that makes us suffer can be replaced by a new positive thought. Now a thought that says, "You never do anything right!" can be turned into "I can handle anything!" Those voices from the past are untruths.

AFFIRM WHO YOU REALLY ARE

Affirmations are positive statements about yourself, which your subconscious now takes in as truth. Our subconscious mind takes in as truth whatever we think or verbalize. This is why we must take those voices from our past that we internalized repeatedly, sometimes thousands of times over a lifetime, and shift them to a true interpretation of ourselves.

Develop an affirmation—a short, positive statement—which you can repeat that really speaks to you. Short, positive phrases that you can repeat are empowering and fill you with potent and vital energy *now*—at this moment. Repeat affirmations with feeling and conviction in the morning ten times and ten times again at night, either aloud or to yourself. These are the hours when your mind is more open and receptive. Within two months of daily consistent practice, affirmations become ingrained in your subconscious and become true facts you naturally "know."

Repeating affirmations daily can also take away attention from those unwanted thoughts that burden you, healing you mentally and emotionally, which, in turn, can potentially heal you physically. Short, empowering, positive phrases become like medicine with no side effects. They energize and revitalize, contributing to a new self-esteem and enthusiasm.

Write, think, or say aloud short, positive affirmations in every area of your life: I wake up energized and eager to start a new day. I have caring and supportive relationships. I have unlimited abundance. Consider areas of your life in which you feel self-doubt and negativity and then rewrite them into positive statements that you can repeat and incorporate during your day. They should feel comfortable as you say them, repeating them easily with meaning and feeling. As you practice affirming positively in every area you find lacking, in two months you will feel empowered, invigorated, and renewed.

Let's say you are feeling self-doubt about a project you have been given at your workplace. You may not hear your self-doubt, but if you are experiencing worry or dread about the project, turn the negative thoughts into positive affirmations. Repeat, "I handle everything well," or "I am doing a great job on the project." Filling your mind with positive affirmations and, at the same time, releasing the negative self-doubt through lack of attention, provides a much-needed enthusiasm and excitement. Now, you *will* handle the project well, and you *will* do a great job.

Begin affirming in every area of your life, releasing all self-doubt. You will acquire a whole new belief system as you turn old, negative beliefs into firm, positive statements! Affirmations should begin with "I have," "I am," "I do," or any statement referring to this moment as if you already have it. You have an amazing power through imagination and feeling to magnetize and bring into your reality whatever you write, think, or say.

When you become aware of a negative thought, say or think, "That's not true," and replace it with a positive thought or affirmation. When you become a more positive person, you release stress from your physical body. A shift to positive emotions is like a fuel, a nutrient. Shifting from negative to positive not only improves our health, it enhances our outlook, attracting better circumstances and situations into our life. Remember that as you become positive, your brain is being reshaped and restructured.

Shifting to being positive is being proactive rather than reactive to life. When we are proactive, we are in charge of our life, keeping our mind positive. As we remember the past, we only remember the good feelings we experienced that can empower us today. When we react in a stressful, anxious way about how something has turned out or what someone has done or said, we are not in charge of our own life. When we react to how someone *is* or how something *turns out* and depend on its outcome in order to be happy, someone or something else is running our life. We are not in control when we are reliant on someone else's either good or bad mood. We are not in control when a situation we cannot change has an emotional impact on us.

You take control and are in charge of your life the moment you actively and *purposefully* think upbeat and feel positive. At that moment, you direct your thoughts to a higher energy, *empowering yourself.*

Neuroscientist Dr. Richard Davidson said, "Even a warm-hearted conversation with a loved one in the morning can structurally modify the brain." He describes how being purposefully positive helps areas in the brain that were once hyperactive, filled with "gibberish," now become "clear as a calm lake."

Often, we think something positive about someone. Why not look for opportunities to express it? People welcome good, heartfelt, and sincere comments about what they are wearing or something they've done or said. People often answer with, "You made my day!" And it's true. Sometimes we give compliments sparingly, keeping to ourselves positive and sincere thoughts about others. Why not express higher-energy thoughts that can go out to others, injecting the higher energy of positive and uplifting feelings into our environment.

Always consider the good qualities of others. Rather than focusing on the negative, "You never [fill in the blank]" or "you always [fill in the blank]," which opens the door to negativity and always hurts, re-enforce only the positive qualities of others. People rise up to what others consider good qualities in themselves, sometimes dissolving whatever "bad" qualities they or others may think they have. When we focus on only the good, the "bad" diminishes.

An easy way to feel positive is to consider all the ways your life feels comfortable, peaceful, easy, and fun. We overlook and mostly never acknowledge life's good moments, especially the ones that make us *feel* good: waking up to a new day, the warm drink that helps us start our day, our coworker's thoughtfulness as we walk into our workplace, a stranger's warm acknowledgment, or getting together for an enjoyable family meal.

By simply acknowledging these moments as they happen throughout your day, you are letting go of negativity and no longer wallowing in self-pity, dread, or fear. You are also helping your brain rebuild itself. Being appreciative is a very powerful force. Besides releasing the negative, you invite more of what you appreciate to come into your life. There is so much power in simply being appreciative! So start a habit of silently appreciating everything that brings you comfort and a good feeling throughout your day to create distance from negativity. The energy of appreciation is one of the highest in the universe and will reflect back into your life whatever you appreciate as situations that seem to unfold perfectly.

Put a notebook with a pen at your bedside and write all the good that transpired during the day. You will be calming the unsatisfied, hard-to-please voice inside you that says, "I never get what I want," or "nothing ever goes my way." The unsatisfied, unhappy, and disgruntled voice will be silenced as you list all that you appreciate.

When you hear the nagging, insistent, negative voice that hammers for your attention, put attention instead on the firm voice of affirmations that makes statements of truth.

MANTRAS CONTAIN THE HIGHER ENERGY WE SEEK

Mantras, or chants, have been used for thousands of years. Early yoga practitioners felt the vibrational energies as they quieted their minds and matched corresponding sounds. The power of mantras and chants is naturally built into the imprint of syllables to which millions before have set a tone and emitted sound in high energy. Chants and mantras are like a comfortable, well-worn pathway, journeyed and energized by millions before us that feel safe, sheltering, and empowering. They carry a high energy of good feelings and good intentions.

Probably the most well-known chant is AUM, which contains three syllables that represent different aspects of Consciousness. It can be repeated for any comfortable length of time. Breathe deeply and emit the elongated sounds that correspond to each syllable of AUM: emit an elongated "awe" for a comfortable length, then "ooh" (comfortable length), and finally "mmm," for a comfortable length. As you bring your lips and teeth together on the final sound of "mmm," you may feel the vibrational energy of AUM.

The high energy of mantras is a safe haven, a protector, shielding you from negativity's damaging effects. Those who are fortunate to feel the subtle vibrational energies can feel the vibrational energy of mantras and chants.

Prayers and chants of all spiritual teachings contain the same high-vibrational sound affecting our energies in a positive way. The "Our Father," as well as the "Ave Maria" in Christianity, also carries the same high vibration, as do mantras and chants from the East.

An easy way to overcome negativity as you notice it is through sounding your note. Each of us has a unique sound that we can emit and find, like a frequency, harmony, and note. Singing is a good way to find a sound that gives you peace, comfort, and a joyous feeling. Your aware attention on the sound you are emitting will release all negativity.

While in this chapter you learned to transform a negative mind of lower energy to a positive mind of higher energy, the mind is still "busy" and still in a dualistic mind pattern, going from negativity to positivity. However, once your mind is more positive, you will find it easier to transition to the serene stillness of the highest energy of Consciousness, where fewer and fewer unwanted thoughts make their way into your inner space. Consciousness is a great power right in the middle of the dualistic nature of negativity and positivity. The silent, still center of yourself, strangely enough, and probably by design, is in the *heart of your Self.*

The next chapter will take you into the still, quiet, and powerful space of the light of Consciousness.

PRACTICES AND SUMMARY
OF CHAPTER THREE

EMPOWERING YOURSELF

1. Look at your surroundings, and create a habit of looking only for the best of life: the best intentions of people, the beauty of nature, even the weather. You are keeping your mind busy on the positive as you let go of negativity.

2. Be gentle as you notice a negative thought coming into your space. Say "thinking" without getting involved in the content of the thought. It will easily dissolve through a lack of attention on it.

3. Look for areas in your life where you have self-doubt and negative beliefs, thoughts, feelings, and emotions. Rewrite them into positive affirmations that you can repeat often.

4. At the end of the day, think about or write down all the experiences throughout the day that you felt good about and can now appreciate. You are opening and becoming receptive to attracting more of the same into your life. You are also calming the voice that says, "Nothing ever goes my way."

5. Think positive thoughts. You are in control of your life the moment you have purposeful and deliberate positive thoughts. At that moment, you are empowering yourself, and your life!

6. Do the high-frequency energies of the mantra AUM, your own unique sound, or repeat a prayer to increase your energy to a higher vibration. This is an easy way to let go of unwanted thoughts, raising the energy of emotional and mental states.

7. Keep in mind that every moment that a positive thought enters your mind, you are benefitting your brain—and your life!

8. Look over past events in your life as connected events, not separate. As you do, you have a better understanding of how certain events that you considered "bad" were actually stepping stones to something better. Seeing past events as connected helps you to see future events in a more favorable light.

SUMMARY

1. In as short a time as an hour and a half, the brain can begin to restructure and rewire itself as you become more positive.

2. By deliberately and purposefully being more positive, you can rewire your brain to help you be a more positive person in the future.

3. The most important aspect of being purposefully positive is that you are now in control of your life, guiding it in the direction you want. You are no longer enslaved by an out-of-control mind. You are in charge!

Chapter Four

THE LIGHT OF CONSCIOUSNESS: YOUR BIRTHRIGHT

The light of Consciousness is the spacious clarity
through which the wondrous and the miraculous enter

We all enter this world in the light of Consciousness—for Consciousness *is* light. We take our first breath, awaken in full awareness, ready to experience life. Each of us came from darkness into light, free of the emotionally draining thoughts that could rob life of its purest and most chaste moments.

LIGHT IS LIFE FORCE ENERGY

Throughout human history, light has always been a symbol of purity and wisdom. Light is a life force energy that heals, warms, and evolves.

In Spanish and Italian, "dar a luz," or "dare alla luz," which is how you say "to give birth," means "to give light." Many cultures around the world celebrate birth in a multitude of ways, all in full agreement of its marvel and wonder.

THE BREATH IS LIGHT

To say that birth is "giving light" gives us insight as to what degree "light" actually influences life. Our life would not be possible without the energetic light of our sun. Light is life itself, the true wealth of life. All life comes from darkness into light: from the roots of plants, deep in the soil, to the perfection and beauty of a flower opening to the light; from the tiny acorn seed turning into the magnificent oak tree, nourished by sunlight; from the baby bird's tiny eye first glimpsing the light of day from its hatched egg; the baby's first breath in the light.

In our vocabulary, to "see the light" means wisdom; it is an expression of seeing more clearly, having better insight, and doing the "right thing." Light translates into light-heartedness and lightness of spirit—not weighed down with despair or depression, nor in a slump because things did not happen in the way we wanted. Light in our everyday vocabulary points to everything that is good—and virtuous.

The lighter we feel within, the more we revive and replenish our spirit. This energetic light helps us let go of what weighs and depresses our spirit. The life force energy of light is accessed through the doorway of our breath, which strengthens, supports, and sustains our life, changing us from the inside out.

THE BREATH IS LOVE

"There is infinitely more to light than we realize… that soft luminosity (is) love itself," author Eckhart Tolle wrote in *The Power of Now*.

As babies, we took in colors, shapes, lights, shadows, and textures to a point of fascination, without cynicism, judgments, or labels. A continual sense of wonder and curious marvel prevailed, from taste, touch, and smell sensations to the excitement of sights and sound. Life was full, whole, and complete, with the freshness, wonder, and awe of life.

To be so aware you are carried on the rhythm of your breath and so alert you reside in the depth of your being is to feel the vast inner being that is *you* in full Consciousness. *Awareness* is who you really are. You have within you a natural, spiritual light.

For millennia, mystics, masters, and sages in the East found Consciousness to be immeasurable and vast, yet something they could reflect on and feel. And *feel* they did. Through the doorway of the breath, they found a powerful and limitless space within each of us that is *felt* as we align with Source, capturing a peaceful, calm, and silent mind.

Science cannot agree on when a baby reaches Consciousness, if at all. However, science measures, weighs, and sees; it cannot *feel*.

THE BREATH IS LIFE ITSELF

Our inner dimension begins with our breath, the sustenance of life. Imagine taking several breaths and suddenly not being able to take another. Would your "problems" still be perceived as insurmountable at that moment? The significance of breath, of life itself, cannot compare to the small, paltry, and insubstantial lower-energy thoughts and problems that continually try to steal us away from our breath. Come home to your breath, to what sustains, nourishes, supports, and ultimately, can heal you.

We breathe unconsciously as we engage in unconscious, unwanted thoughts, emotions, and feelings that generate shallow and unsteady breathing, making us feel uneasy and disharmonious. As we become aware and conscious of our breath in calm relaxation, we quiet and calm the mind and create harmonious, flowing, easy breathing.

YOUR TRUE SELF WILL EMERGE

With a quieter, calmer mind, you will be taken back, once again, to the clean slate, the clear canvas that you were as you came into this physical existence.

Consciousness is life in its most truthful. For what could be truer than your breath as you feel it in this moment? Truer than the stream of life flowing through your hands, arms, legs, and feet, your whole body, *now*? Is your *feeling Self* in this moment not truer than the projections of the mind-made past and future? The mind that continually rehashes what someone said that was interpreted as hurtful? The mind that makes us fearful of a picture we hold of the future? Living in truth is living in the awareness of our centered Self, the heart of our True Self, our true nature, where life becomes less complicated, with less struggle, and more ease.

The more you are aware of yourself within, even a few seconds, the more the light of Consciousness will grow within. Every moment spent consciously aware and attentive of your inner life force, however short the time span—a few seconds— increases your light. Without the heavy weight of unwanted thoughts, light can now make its way in. Author and spiritual teacher Eckhart Tolle wrote in *The Power of Now*, "Every time you create a gap in the stream of mind, the light of your Consciousness grows stronger." The mind needs to be cleared of the pollution of thoughts that do nothing to help you move forward in life. The pollution of thoughts that dishearten and depress your spirit. Once the mind is free of the pollution and waste of unwanted thoughts that bring you down, blocking you from feeling good, you become free from the imprisonment and enslavement of negative thoughts. While the gaps and spaces may only last a few seconds, over time they will last longer, providing increasing freedom from harmful thoughts. You will now be calmer, be more alert, have clarity of mind, and resolve challenges because of a spacious mind.

FROM DARKNESS INTO LIGHT

Light is energy. It is this energy of light that you will use through the practices here to let go and release what now does not make you feel good. The light will help you heal from the low energies that harm your mental, emotional, and physical self.

Ancient texts, for millennia, described the "light" of Consciousness as a healing light. Light will dissolve unwanted thoughts and emotions even if you have not figured out why and where they came from. You can release them and let them go.

Practice: Healing the stress of mental, emotional, and physical pain

If you are feeling stressed through experiencing either physical or emotional pain, the following healing yoga practice, thousands of years old, will heal you:

Sit up straight, relaxing your shoulders, your hands, and the muscles in your face. Imagine that as you inhale through your nose, you are breathing in light, letting it permeate throughout your body. Exhale as if through a straw, slowly, extended and unbroken, releasing all stress, tension, unwanted thoughts, emotions, and feelings. Continue inhaling and exhaling in the same way three or four times or until you feel calm.

By doing this practice, your brain gains the light of Consciousness, creating new neuropathways as toxic stress is released. As you inhale, you are surrounded by the light of Consciousness, lighting up every cell, every part of your being. You are in an energy field of no limitations in your body or mind. You are helping your mental, emotional, and physical bodies heal by doing this practice often, taking just seconds. You will become calmer as you release mental stress and physical harm from your body, feeling better and better in a month or two of daily practice.

Healing can also be experienced through imagining surrounding burdensome thoughts and emotions with light. As you do, you are not fighting thoughts, but dissolving them and turning them into light, without a struggle.

Practice: Surround unwanted thoughts with light

Take a few deep breaths to calm yourself. Inhale three or four seconds, and exhale three or four seconds. Inhale light and imagine it permeating your body from your head to your toes. Exhale out all unwanted thoughts and emotions surrounding them in light. Imagine them dissolving and turning into light.

THE HEALING POWER OF MEDITATION

For millennia, meditation has been a vehicle to alleviate unwanted thoughts and emotions by creating a much-needed space between thoughts. Meditation is simply focusing on your breath, inner life force, or, if you'd like, whatever object of attention you have chosen—whether a flickering candle, a gem, a crystal, a rock, or simply contemplating breath-taking scenery. Remember that what you put attention on grows in your experience and also becomes what you create in life. You are training your mind to be alert, spacious, and aware without stressed, anxious thoughts. And you are practicing bringing back a wandering mind again and again to a calm and peaceful focus, creating a resilient nature.

Beginners should not "push away" or "try to get rid of" thoughts. Once you notice a thought while focusing on your breath, inner Self, or any object, be gentle, calm, and peaceful because fighting and battling thoughts will encourage thoughts to fight back. What you resist will persist. You will then lose the whole purpose of meditation, which is practicing a state of peaceful bliss and calm in non-thought and non-judgment. A way to maintain the peace of meditation is to imagine thoughts like clouds dissolving or balloons floating up to the sky that you tap gently with a feather. In this way, you bring back the mind again and again to a peaceful awareness.

What you are "doing" in meditation turns into "being" in your daily life. You become more at ease and calmer. You become less judgmental and more alert and aware. In daily life, you will now listen better, read with more comprehension, and study with more focus. You are creating space between thoughts, gaining the light of Consciousness and also gaining a newfound peace from what was once a noisy mind. Meditation also improves emotional and physical health, as it helps you release the fearful and angry mind.

Practice: A calming, blissful meditation

Practice the following meditation for five minutes, increasing to ten to fifteen minutes per day if you'd like.

Sit with a focus on your breath or a focus of attention on an object of your choice for three to five minutes, gradually increasing the minutes per day. As you notice a thought, come back again and again to a focus of breath or object. Be gentle as you notice a thought. With no involvement or judgment, imagine thoughts floating up to the sky as you tap them lightly with a feather, or imagine thoughts becoming light as they dissolve.

MEDITATION IS A BLISSFUL STATE OF BEING

As unwanted thoughts lessen, you will feel the blissful state of meditation. When you do reach this rich space of being blissful, you will no longer have to rely on an object of focus. You will simply sit with a quiet, still mind and feel bliss! Feeling bliss in non-thought is the essence of meditation.

THE LIGHT OF CONSCIOUSNESS

THE FEARFUL AND
WEAK SHADOWY ENTITY

Ancient texts and modern-day spiritual teachers have described the phenomenon of the mind of unwanted thoughts as a shadowy "false" entity, fearing losing its life in the light. And this is true! The light it fears is the light of your Consciousness! This false, shadowy entity is fearful and weak in your powerful presence. The light of your Consciousness can easily dissolve darkness. We see it every day as the sun rises, easily and gently "blanketing" the darkness. The darkness that depresses you is weak and dissolves easily through light.

Depressive thoughts and the stressful and painful emotions they produce cannot be overcome through more "thinking," more darkness. When you are thinking about a problem through a confused, frustrated mind, you will only circle again and again without a solution. The confused, unconscious mind dissolves easily as you imagine the light of your breath turning this unconscious mind into light. There is nothing to fight, think about, or conflict with. The darkness of thoughts and emotions that do not make you feel good have no chance as you practice and increasingly gain light.

BE THE CHANGE THE WORLD NEEDS

The light of Consciousness can be spread as easily as contagious laughter or a contagious smile. Today, humanity needs the light of Consciousness more than ever—to soothe, restore, and heal ourselves and our planet. You, as part of the human collective, can help. Every moment you feel uplifted, revitalized, strengthened, and appreciative is a powerful energy that infiltrates the environment and helps heal the planet. Imagine each of us as a cell in the body of Mother Earth. As more of us gain the vibrant life force energies of Consciousness, the "body" of our planet, with which we are so connected, shares in the life force vibrancy and heals.

As we nurture and develop Consciousness, a beautiful and burgeoning growth appears. Like the apple on a tree and a rose on a bush, flourishing qualities are exposed: compassion, loving kindness, peace, cooperation, and joy—all qualities that could shield humanity from war, pestilence, hatred, divisions, and limitations.

The light of Consciousness is a thousand times more powerful than the negativity infiltrating our world today. Like a beacon of light, you can now help a world in jeopardy by simply being consciously aware.

Life was not meant to be as problematic and challenging as we make it. The light of Consciousness will open you to inner peace and calmness. You will emerge lighter in spirit and more powerful than ever to touch, open, and influence an outside world.

YOUR BIRTHRIGHT:
THE LIGHT OF CONSCIOUSNESS

1. Practice: Healing the stress of mental, emotional, and physical pain

If you are feeling stressed through experiencing either physical or emotional pain, the following healing yoga practice thousands of years old will heal you:

Sit up straight, relaxing your shoulders, your hands, and the muscles in your face. Imagine that as you inhale through your nose, you are breathing in light, letting it permeate throughout your body. Exhale as if through a straw, slowly, extended and unbroken, releasing all stress, tension, unwanted thoughts, emotions, and feelings. Continue inhaling and exhaling in the same way, three or four times, or until you feel calm.

2. Practice: A calming, blissful meditation

Remember to relax completely, immersed in a feeling of bliss as you meditate. As thoughts appear, be gentle by allowing them to dissolve into light. Allow meditation to heal you by creating space between thoughts:

Sit with a focus on your breath or on any object of your choice for three to five minutes, gradually increasing the minutes per day. As you notice a thought, come back again and again to a focus of breath or object. Be gentle as you notice a thought. With no judgment or involvement, imagine thoughts dissolving into light, or imagine thoughts like balloons floating up to the sky as you tap them lightly with a feather.

3. Practice: Dissolving unwanted thoughts with light

Another way to dissolve burdensome thoughts is through light: Take a few deep breaths to feel calm. Inhale three or four seconds, then exhale three or four seconds. Inhale light from your head to your toes. Exhale out all unwanted thoughts and burdens, surrounding them in light and imagining them dissolving into light.

4. Light force energy can be accessed through your breath in calm relaxation. Practice awareness of your breath, and imagine useless low energies dissolving.

5. Be conscious of your breath to create harmony and balance in your life. The mind of unconscious thoughts produces unconscious breathing that is shallow and unsteady, making you feel unbalanced and uneasy.

SUMMARY

1. Light is a powerful life force energy. This is a healing light that can help you let go of low energies that harm you mentally and physically.

2. Your breath is life itself, what sustains and nourishes you. The low energies like stress, anxiety, fear, and anger are weak, small, and meaningless in relation to the light of your life-giving breath.

3. The darkness of harmful thoughts and emotions has no chance in your life force energetic light. There is nothing to think about or have conflict with; your inner light will dissolve harmful thoughts and emotions as you are relaxed, calm, and peaceful.

4. As part of the human collective, you can help heal humanity and the planet as you feel uplifted, revitalized, and strengthened.

Chapter Five

FINDING YOURSELF

You find yourself within your rhythmic flowing heart

Y ou have now practiced opening to Consciousness through
attention on your inner Self where there *are no problems*.
The more you connect with your life force energy within, in
peace and calm, the freer you will be from unwanted thoughts
of the past and future, and the more clarity you will gain. Your
perspective of "problems" that present themselves will change.
Little by little, you will realize that what you once considered a
problem is really a helpful situation. With more spaciousness
and more clarity of mind, you will now be open to insightful
ideas and revelations to help you find a solution to a
challenging situation.

Inspirational ideas and revelations make their appearance more
and more often when the mind of unwanted thoughts is less
evident. Eventually, you will "know" if an idea is the perfect

solution to a challenge, and you will welcome an inspirational idea with pleasure and reverence. These insightful ideas are like golden nuggets, helping you to move forward in your life. However, these insightful ideas are not scarce and limited; they are abundant, and they come through a more spacious mind.

Until you gain more Consciousness, you might still experience a "problem" in the same anxious way that is considered normal. However, every second you spend creating gaps and spaces in your mind is a second that will move your life toward that which is your highest good.

Do not be hard on yourself for feeling that you are still struggling with unwanted thoughts and the problems they produce. It takes time to free your mind from the immersion and involvement in the drama of life. You are practicing here to see only the best of what life offers. You are practicing a joyful acceptance of life at each moment. However, we are constantly in the midst of a world that considers problems to be a natural occurrence in everyday life. That is hard to escape, so congratulate and appreciate yourself for the effort and accomplishment you make day to day to transition to a more joyful experience of life. This simple congratulatory appreciation of yourself can raise your energetic field, taking you far beyond the mind of anguish and difficulties.

When someone says, "I have to find myself," the roots of these words come from non-acceptance, resistance, fight, and battle with their present life experience, causing fear, anger, anxiety, and stress. An event that stirs us to want to "find" ourselves usually concerns some loss. Whether we lose a job, money, a relationship, our health, or a loved one, each of us experiences several losses, in different degrees, that can be catalysts for change. Like the silver lining in a dark cloud, a challenging loss can shift our way of thinking and awaken us to a different way of being, freeing us. The unraveling of a deep personal loss awakens us to the realization that reality was not what we thought. It may feel like falling through an abyss and being caught before we hit rock bottom.

A GROWTH OPPORTUNITY

Being caught before we hit bottom means opening to transformation, bringing about a great opportunity for growth. It is as if our raw emotions are opened and exposed to new, higher energies that abound. The opportunity may come about in a chance encounter with someone or something that can help. You may hear someone say something that triggers a new insight or find a book or an article that can help.

Look for wide-open doors that seem to reach out to you. You can open to a path of Consciousness, a different perspective, a new way of being. Or you could wallow in self-pity, remorse, and regret in a never-ending cycle of drawbacks, obstacles, and difficulties that reflect back into your life as situations, mirroring the same low energy you are generating.

Whatever personal problem you experience simply means you can now fix what needed fixing. The darkness of a loss in our life is what propels and inspires us to want to seek the light. This is how a challenge that you experience as the "worst thing that can possibly happen" can actually be "very good news," as one Eastern sage calls life's challenges.

Another bit of good news is that you do not need a challenging situation to seek the light. You can open *now* to a path of Consciousness, of being consciously aware, without having to experience an overwhelming loss. Far better to begin now, at this moment.

Practice: Allow "problems" to pass through a transparent you

When a "problem" feels overwhelming, you want to run away and not feel its pain. By allowing it to "pass through" a transparent you, *feeling* the energy of the emotional pain but not the content, you can dissolve it.

Sit in a comfortable position as soon as an overwhelming feeling of sadness from the past or worry about the future overcomes you. Stay with the feeling, not thinking about it, indulging in it, or judging it. Allow the energetic feeling of the sadness or worry to "loving-kindness" you, imagining yourself transparent and it "passing" through you.

Staying with the energy of the feeling of this kind of emotional pain is important. Stay with the feeling with no indulgence and no judgment. Allowing the energies of unwanted thoughts and emotions to "go through" a transparent you may be the true and inherent meaning of the saying "and this too shall pass."

Author Pema Chodron, in *When Things Fall Apart*, described the process as "allow[ing] it to pierce you in the heart." Simply stay with the energy of a feeling until it passes through. Eventually, these thoughts and emotions will dissolve, and they will lose their power over you, never bothering you again.

"I have to find myself" really means "I have to find peace." Instinctively, we go toward the soothing qualities of nature. We may wander through a park and, for the first time, watch the dance of leaves on a tree, notice the streaks of sunlight on the grass, and feel the soft breeze on our face. We become suddenly *awakened* to life all around us. This is how a problem or challenge we encounter as "terrible" can be a new opportunity to open to life, as we experience aliveness through our sense perceptions of sight, sound, smell, taste, and touch. It is also life in its most pure, authentic, and genuine form, free of problems, stresses, and anxieties—very much how life was meant to be lived. Most importantly, it is living in the only place life truly exists—now, at this moment—free of emotional pain. You will learn more about the power of "the present moment" in a later chapter.

We find ourselves in the natural world, the forms of nature, the beauty of trees, flowers, lakes, and mountains. And we can also find ourselves in the simple acceptance of life surrounding us at this moment. In those moments, we find the heart of ourselves.

We also find ourselves through the ebb and flow of our natural world within—the life force of our breath, life flowing through our inner Self, feeling life flowing and streaming within. As we do this, we leave behind suffering, anxiety, and stress in the still and peaceful awareness we create. We now move easily between the quiet spaces of our world within and our newly formed positive experience of an outside world.

CLOSING OUR HEART TO LIFE

There are many instances in which we close up. A relationship may not be going as well as was anticipated. We close if someone we love says or does something we do not like. The heart is like an energy valve that opens and closes. When we become immersed in circling, hurtful, low-energy thoughts, we close, and it becomes another energy block among many in our heart. An accumulation of blockages prevents energy from coming through and throws it into darkness, closing it off. Imagine a river clogged with debris. It becomes stagnant and immobile, no longer vibrantly alive. Once the river is cleared of debris, its vibrancy comes back, and a whole life-giving ecosystem flows naturally again.

Everything should pass through the heart easily. Life is not being lived how it was meant to be lived if you keep closing your heart. Imagine yourself with an open heart that never closes. You would be accepting life in each moment in whatever form it presented itself—with no judgment. It does not mean that you have to like everything that happens, only that through non-judgment, it does not affect you. You are at peace and not in a continuous battle and fight with life.

An open heart translates into an acceptance of life no matter what transpires. An accepting, open heart means liking life, no matter how life unfolds. When we live like this, it is as if we are rewarded. We get back more of the same that we are accepting and, therefore, appreciating. We also do not have to worry about trying to control every situation. Eventually, situations and circumstances unfold in a better way. As we become aware of life, while we drive and do tasks and chores around our home, accidents greatly diminish. Conflicts are lessened because, with an open heart, we are not judgmental of what someone says or does that before may have been interpreted negatively. Life then works in our favor. As we trust and don't hold on so tightly by trying to control every situation, an energy of peace radiates out to others. Through calm relaxation and in-the-moment acceptance, you will find an open heart, easily and effortlessly.

Eventually, life will get easier—less complicated—as each occurrence, like yourself, becomes friendlier, more approachable. Imagine yourself simply watching with no judgment as your family learned life's lessons on their own. You would certainly become more approachable if they decided they needed your help. You would now come from more clarity and non-judgment. As you changed, every area of your life would also change—for the better.

Rumi wrote poetic, timeless words in the thirteenth century that apply more than ever to our twenty-first-century life:

"Out beyond ideas of wrongdoing and right doing, there is a field.

I'll meet you there.

When the soul lies down in that grass

The world is too full to talk about."

Decide that you are going to open to life. Your decision to open whole-heartedly in your daily life will help you find that field of which Rumi speaks. It is an open, energetic field with the warming and healing properties of peace. It is a field out beyond the talk that separates and divides. Life is simple, uncomplicated, and filled with the energy of light. It is a field where there are no disagreements, no discord. Neither is there a world too "fool" to talk about.

Rumi speaks of being in a calm, timeless energy field, where you are in your heart, beyond the mind of right and wrong. Within a silent heart, you can now delight in the simple pleasure of basking in the warmth of the sun. Life is whole and complete.

Closing to life limits the way you will accept events that happen to you, making you feel boxed in and constantly worrying about closing down when things don't "fit in" with your interpretation of how things "should be." Accepting everything just as it is in each moment means never having to worry about what happens and having to control it. You are watching life—its dance and its flows—as it unfolds.

It does *not* mean, however, accepting something in your life that you do not like or want. When we face an overwhelming situation where we can't seem to find our footing, it becomes doubly important to keep the pollution of worry, anxiety, and stress from entering our space.

You have within these pages many tools that you can use to protect your inner space from the onslaught and pollution of an outside world. If you cannot find joy in a challenging situation, you *can* find peace!

A situation that immerses you in anxiety and stress can be changed through a decision and intent to want to transform a low-energy feeling to one that contains a higher-energy, better feeling. Once you decide to have the intent to be or to do something in a different way, you empower yourself because a positive intent is a one-pointed, focused decision you have made to change something for the better. In the same moment that you consider a positive intent, your brain will follow suit by cooperating as it continues restructuring itself.

Remember that the doorway to your heart is through your breath. An aware, easy flow of breath is important moment to moment, appreciating and finding only beauty in our surroundings, in nature, in what we love to do.

Life can be filled with challenges, some very difficult. However, when you are faced with an overwhelming challenge, stand back to gain a better view of the big picture of your life. The more you stand back to view the big picture of your life, the more clarity you will gain. How can this challenge actually help you? Sometimes things happen that can actually be beneficial. In the case of a job loss, for instance, perhaps you never enjoyed the job anyway. This is a good opportunity to do something for a living that is more enjoyable.

When a challenging situation arises needing your immediate attention, as you gain Consciousness, you will come from a place of calm and clarity. As you live more and more in Consciousness, you will now come from the composure and tranquility of your True Self, with no mental pollution, and better understand you do the best you can under the circumstances. You will have more clarity about whether to remove yourself from the situation or have the wisdom to understand what to do about the situation.

Soon enough, those "problems" and challenges will change, becoming softer, easier. And this has to do with living in the natural flow of your energy field, a place beyond the destructive and menacing forces of problems that our culture seems to think is normal.

HOLDING ON TO PAIN

You may have kept every hurtful thing ever said to you by anyone—a parent, a teacher, another child who simply might have been experiencing a bad day—inside for days, months, years, maybe even a lifetime, producing a blockage of emotional pain. "You never do anything right!" "You're not pretty enough." "Your artwork was the worst one!" "You're always..." or "You'll never..." The list is as endless as there are people. If you experienced being bullied by another, more unconscious child, you may have been told to "hit back," or you may have been told you being picked on "must be your fault."

These hurtful words are like voices kept in our minds. It is energy lodged, very often in our hearts. These negative energies produce an imprint, like well-worn tracks in our minds. Blockage and obstruction is formed that stunts our mental and emotional growth and keeps us from moving forward.

However, whether we interpret energy as "good" or "bad," it is life energy, nonetheless, and can be used as another tool to help us heal. We can practice becoming transparent and simply allow the energy of a "bad" feeling to pass through, as we so naturally seemed to do as a young child. Allow a negative feeling to "pass through" a transparent you, without judgment, without involvement in the content of an unwanted thought.

The feeling of loss, of someone or something, are also blockages produced as we hold on to intense emotional pain. This emotional pain can lead to health issues, arising someplace in your physical body. A health issue that comes from emotional pain can make its appearance weeks or months after a traumatic event. Through persistently practicing the tools you have been given and are available within yourself at this moment, the emotional pain of the loss can be released more and more through a cumulative effect. Your physical body will now be relieved of the stress caused by emotional pain.

Feelings that depress and sadden come through in an instant. They come in through our senses, not through a thought. They are feelings that come through in an instant, catching us off-guard. Suddenly smelling the perfume of the loved one we lost, hearing a song we once shared with someone special, or seeing the same color and form of a dress or shirt that reminds us of a past event, can create an instant hurtful feeling within. You can learn to allow the painful feeling, which is not a thought, to subside by practicing allowing it to "pass through you," as you learned to do earlier.

To simply allow, observe, and watch for obstacles in our path and easily go around them is like a mighty river maneuvering smooth-edged rocks, representing the many hurdles in life. In the same way, as we clear the debris within, our own life force energy will now flow freely, with more power and less effort.

Eventually, these hurtful feelings will subside, opening your heart. Staying with the feeling of an intense thought and not indulging in its content is important because an intense thought will produce an intense energy charge, leading to a painful emotion. Intense thoughts and intense emotions will produce a vicious cycle of thoughts and emotions circling repeatedly.

Nothing should become lodged nor blocked within. In a natural way, through practice, without fight or battle, you will "let go" of hurtful and harmful thoughts and emotions. Observe and notice an unwanted thought neutrally, with no judgment. The power inherent in our ability to "observe" will be explored more in a later chapter.

While your newfound peace from emotional upheaval and a noisy mind is reward enough, the more profound reward comes from the boundless depths of an energetic space that is now freed, opening to a life of more ease and much less struggle.

We believe we have to go away to find peace from too much thinking. However, peace can be found in the calm, rhythmic flow within our heart.

You will find yourself in the depths of your heart, "out beyond the talk of right or wrong." Your heart is the energetic field of ease, peace, and joy. You will no longer be reliving past pain nor have fear of what the future holds. The True You was there all along; the clear sky filled with light, always there, just behind stormy clouds.

FINDING YOURSELF

1. As soon as you feel a weighed down and depressed feeling, *sit in a comfortable position and allow the energy of the pain to "pass through you." Imagine yourself transparent, allowing only the energy of it, not the content, without thought and without indulgence, to pass through a transparent you.* Stay with the energy of the feeling until it passes through you, gradually subsiding. Soon it will lose its power over you and dissolve for good.

2. Go toward the soothing qualities of nature, either in person or in your imagination. Calm yourself through your breath. With no labels or scientific names, *feel* the essence, the fundamental nature, of a flower or a tree. Connect with yourself within, taking deep breaths as you feel the peace and calm. Move easily between your peaceful inner world and an alive and vibrant natural world.

3. Practice having an open heart in your daily life. Live in full acceptance and awareness of all that surrounds you.

SUMMARY

1. Connecting to your life force energy in peace and calm will help you to have a more spacious mind. You will have more clarity to solve challenges and realize that a challenge can be a helpful situation.

2. Do not be hard on yourself for feeling that you are still struggling with unwanted thoughts and the challenges they produce. Every second you spend creating gaps and spaces in between your thoughts will move your life forward.

3. Whatever loss you experience can be a catalyst for positive change. You can now fix what needed fixing, and a loss can inspire you to want to seek the light.

4. Nothing should become lodged nor blocked within your heart. Without a fight or battle, simply let go of hurtful and harmful feelings through the doorway of your breath.

Chapter Six

AWARENESS AND
VIBRANT ALIVENESS

A clear and pure mind celebrates life

As a baby, your alert awareness was on your inner being and life coming in through your five senses. It was one moment in your life when you were most conscious and aware, totally present in your felt senses, without judgment, cynicism, or self-doubt, all within a quiet mind.

Having awareness in non-thought is a key to how you can free yourself from the imprisonment of problems produced from the thoughts and emotions of fear, tension, stress, anger, self-pity, guilt, and loneliness—an endless range of low-energy feelings. The way you came into this world is a hint that the mind of thoughts is not needed. Or, more accurately, the neurotic mind of useless, low-energy thoughts is not needed.

You *can* live peacefully and joyfully in non-thought. As a baby, you were very happy taking in the world all around you simply observing and accepting life!

Can you imagine living without thought? You might say it really can't be done, that it's impossible to live without thoughts. You might even be inclined to say that you would be more like a vegetable in a world where the thought process is king, an intellectual standard. Most societies around the world, especially in western cultures, value the "intellectual" properties of the mind. Education and the ability to create a living at its highest monetary levels take a very important role in most western cultures.

However, we are referring to unwanted thoughts that have become addictive and destructive, reflecting more and more in every area of our society. Our highly productive mind is priceless when used in creative and practical ways rather than in the emotional way of the relentless "my story." Giving attention to our story of a painful past and a fearful future keeps us from the peace and joy we seek.

The mind, used in the right way, is very helpful. It becomes greatly enhanced, however, as you distance yourself from the high percentage of thoughts that are not at all beneficial. These constant unbeneficial thoughts are what impair and weaken our entire existence as they entrap and ensnare us through the attention we put on them. Once we purposefully diminish these detrimental thoughts that don't help us move forward, the mind is greatly enhanced!

The mind becomes sharper and gains clarity as we use it in a practical way to do tasks, errands, chores, solve math problems, study, cook, drive, and plan our future. When we perform tasks in fully focused attention, the mind is more at peace and can help us do whatever needs to be done in a faster and more efficient way.

Our mind also becomes more creative as we expand our Consciousness, capturing creative insight and inspiration that reaches beyond our analytical, linear mind. All beauty in the world comes from the creative mind. The dance, the poem, and the melody that resonate with our heart come from this creative mind. The linear, analytical mind does not deviate, staying transfixed on a line between point A and point B. Amazingly, as we become more consciously aware, our sharper and quicker mind taps into the creative mind that is beyond our everyday mind. We are then given inspiration and insight into something we put aware attention on that seems to magically arise because our mind is so clear!

As we gain Consciousness through a quiet and aware mind, we are no longer solely reliant on the knowledge we've accumulated in our lifetime. We now open to a vaster, immeasurable Creative Intelligence, a powerful force, a resource of insight and inspiration on any subject of our choosing. Both Einstein and Tesla recognized this resource of information that they could tap into as they rested and relaxed without thought and found solutions they had previously pursued through a "thinking mind."

Once you are your Self in Consciousness, alert and aware of your inner Self without thought, the mind is very much at peace and becomes an enhanced tool that helps greatly as you do anything not involving "my story." Once the mind begins a conversation of your "story," *beware.* They are unwanted thoughts coming from the false mind, threatening your freedom, your peaceful sanctuary, your safe haven, your health, and your life!

You will learn more about the false "ego-mind" of unwanted thoughts as you read the next chapter. The unwanted thoughts dissolved through the practices here are those that loop and circle worries, stress, anxieties, past pain, and all negativity. They are useless, unproductive thoughts that do not move our life forward.

Today, many suffer from looping thoughts: the ones that circle repeatedly and go around again and again in the head with no solution. When it involves thinking about a past problem, it leads to guilt, anger, remorse, and regret. When it involves thinking about the future, it leads to worry, anxiety, stress, tension, and dread. As the mind loops the problem again and again, the clutter and chaos going on in the mind prevents a real and positive solution.

Yet the mind continues relentless and overwhelmed, and if unchecked, can harm mental and physical health and will very quickly "take you over," enslaving you. The mind, then, takes an addictive form. We no longer have the choice to stop thinking.

When thoughts become addictive, producing problems with no expectation of a solution to escape the chaos in our mind, we may find a "solution" through another addictive means, like food, alcohol, drugs, work, or shopping; an endless list that further complicates life. Now we have two addictions: the addictive mind we cannot control that has enslaved and imprisoned us, and the added addiction we think will save us from an out-of-control, addictive mind. Today, many have not only two addictions, but also three and even four or more. The addiction of the mind is the underlying cause of all other addictions. All addictions are used as an escape from a mind that makes us feel as if we are being driven crazy.

Addiction means not having a choice to stop. As you practice being consciously aware of your Self within, you will have no more "out-of-control thinking." Through conscious self-awareness, you may choose to stop addictive thinking. You are no longer taken over and enslaved by an out-of-control mind. Unwanted thoughts will simply stop through a lack of attention on them. It will be gradual, but with intent and practice, you will achieve distancing yourself from unwanted thoughts, naturally curing addictive thinking.

The actual root of all addictions, the mind of thoughts we do not want, may be the most easily overcome. *However, you need real intent and desire to finally overcome your present emotional pain and suffering.*

Freedom from the mind's relentless nature is as close as this moment, in calm and peace. *At every opportunity, become aware of your life force energy within—your breath, the life force streaming through you from your head to your toes, and your surroundings, in positive acceptance. Persistently practicing in this calm place within* will now open the possibility for *all addictions to fall away. With the mind of harmful thoughts no longer there, you now have no reason to escape!*

The next time you reach for a sweet you know is not good for you or any comfort food you consider detrimental to your health and weight, *stop!* What was the chain of thoughts that made you want to seek comfort? Were they stressful and anxious thoughts of what the future may hold, or were they thoughts filled with remorse and sadness about an event you may still hold on to from the past?

When you substantially reduce thoughts and go about your day only using thoughts you need (like remembering an appointment or doing a task), and then when you're finished come back to a mind without useless and detrimental thoughts, it will be much easier to feel the thoughts that brought you to a moment of stress, anxiety, pain, or sadness. As you practice putting undivided attention on a new recipe, a math problem, a new language, cleaning house, washing up, anything that moves life in the direction you want, you will think more clearly, actually doing a better job in a faster time frame! You will also be less inclined to do and reach for that which is not good for you!

Michael Singer, author of *The Untethered Soul*, describes the pendulum in which we habitually live. When your attention is on the detrimental thoughts that constantly put you on edge, the pendulum swings slow and wide, wasting precious time.

As you transition to attention and an awareness of life flowing through you, neither yearning nor wanting anything more at this moment, the pendulum would now have more concentrated energy, much less loss of energy, swinging short swings in the middle. With unwanted thoughts no longer there, you would now get more done in less time, feel more whole and complete, feel more fulfilled, and feel more at peace as you open to a new way of life containing infinite possibilities. Thoughts that now come through are from a place of more depth and clarity, giving you inspiration and creative ideas and, increasingly, fulfillment and gratification, leading you to your life's purpose, what you love to do.

Let's examine this further as you imagine that you want to get ahead in your career, and you are doing a special project so you can be promoted.

Not yet practicing Consciousness, as you drive home from work, you are angered by another driver who "cut you off."

Already seething because of a coworker's display of arrogance, you get home tired, exhausted, and irritated. Your normal routine when this happens is to call a friend or rehash the entire day's events with your spouse, believing that retelling the story with all its irritating details will relieve your annoyance. Too tired to work on your special project, you simply fall into bed, dreading another day in the workplace.

You have now had a few months of Consciousness practice. You are at work and the same "annoying" coworker is at it again. This time, you simply feel the energy of the irritation with no indulgence, no judgment, and no thought, allowing it to pass through a transparent you, just as you do at home whenever you experience the same negative thought and emotion. You finish your work on time and leave. You drive home in total awareness. At a stop, you notice the tawny ocher hue of a tree shedding its autumn leaves and smile as you remember the sound of crackling leaves under your feet as a child. With no judgment or labels, you simply take in its beauty and its colors. Your thoughts of the past now only contain the moments in which you felt good and empowered.

You continue fully aware of your driving. At home, your aware attention continues as you do each task, totally aware of what you are doing and nothing else, one thing at a time. The tasks are now done more quickly, more efficiently, and even more joyfully than ever. Once you finish working on your project, you go to bed fully satisfied, and you congratulate yourself on a job well done.

Can you see how your aware, attentive mind went from one task to the next in a flowing, easy manner, no longer encumbered and weighed down by negative thinking? Can you see how letting go of the irritating stuff that wastes precious time and energy can help you move forward? You are no longer enslaved nor dependent on how you feel by what happens in an outside world. You are in full control and have let go by being in full, aware acceptance of life in each moment.

Your power comes from being in aware, focused attention *now*, to create the future. You are in your power, no longer dependent on what others say and do to feel fulfilled and alive. You are the captain of your ship, at the helm of your own life!

Once we put alert and accepting awareness on life in non-thought, with no judgment or cynicism, nothing of a lower energy enters our sacred space. Our mind becomes centered and wise.

There is a new excitement and vibrancy for life. As depressive thoughts cease, you are now captivated once again by life's wonder and freshness, just as you were as a young child. You now have more time and also more spaciousness in your mind to notice the dance of light as it comes in through a window, the aroma of foliage and trees after rain, the graceful soar of birds on windswept currents, all observed in aware non-thought. A feeling of connection to all of nature, your loved ones, everyone, will emerge. Compassion and love will arise when you least expect it. And they *will* arise.

As you practice the processes in this book, you will realize there is no harm, but tremendous advantage as you *substantially reduce thoughts*. The new spaciousness in your mind, now freed of past pain and worry of the future has made room for joy, felt when you have a light-heartedness and vitality for life.

Your increasing peace and compassion, a close link to the energy of love, have the boundlessness and depth of a star-studded night sky. You are whole and complete, connected to a vast and infinite space.

PRACTICES AND SUMMARY
OF CHAPTER SIX

AWARENESS AND VIBRANT ALIVENESS

1. Allow your creative mind to unveil and be revealed. All beauty in the world comes from this mind: the dance, the melody, the visual art. The mind that creates bestows the feelings that come from our innate sense of beauty.

2. As soon as your mind is thinking of the past or the future, beware. These are unwanted thoughts that will lower your energetic life force. The mind of "my story" can harm physical and mental health and very quickly becomes addictive, which means you can no longer stop thoughts.

3. At every opportunity, become aware of your life force energy within. As you do, you are shifting attention away from thoughts and emotions of anger, sadness, stress, anxiety, and fear. *Freedom from the mind's relentless nature is as close as this moment, in calm peace.*

4. Be captivated by life's wonder and freshness. Become aware of your surroundings as if through the eyes of a child. Notice the dance of light as it comes in through a window; the aroma of fresh rain on grass, trees, and foliage; the windswept currents supporting birds in flight.

As you do, you are allowing inner peace and joy to emerge, and you are practicing living life in non-thought, a key that will help you to release detrimental, useless thoughts.

5. Put undivided, aware attention on each task as you do it. Practice a silent awareness as you drive, cook a meal, or study. The mind is helpful as you remember an appointment and is very keen and alert as you study or read.

SUMMARY

1. Living with awareness in non-thought is a key to living free of detrimental thoughts and emotions.

2. Our thinking mind is priceless when used in an aware and focused way. However, the lower energies must be cleared so that we can feel our aliveness.

3. As you release addictive unwanted thoughts, you can now release all other addictions, like food, shopping, and alcohol, because you no longer have a reason to escape!

Chapter Seven

YOU ARE *NOT* *YOUR* THOUGHTS

You are a Boundless, Limitless, and Powerful Being.

In our complex world, we've become so accustomed to persistent, unwanted thoughts that often we cannot even "hear" the mindless dialogue that takes place within, imprisoning and demoralizing us. A high percentage of our thoughts are a never-ending discussion—sometimes we may join in on the conversation—that continues uninterrupted even when there seem to be no problems. It becomes our boss, saying, "Get up, what are you doing?" "You don't have time for that!" "You have so much to do!" "There you go losing the keys again!" "You shouldn't have said that!"

THE DYSFUNCTION:
THE FALSE MIND, THE EGO

Viewing the "ego," and what will be described here as the "false mind," as an entity feeding off you might further influence you to escape its enslavement and imprisonment and be at the helm of your life. The false mind has become like a monstrous entity, addictively holding most of humanity in a feverish tenacity that won't let up. All strife, unhappiness, and discord in the world can be traced back to its malfunction.

The mind we view as an essential part of our lives can be more in line with a tormentor that belittles, abuses, and betrays. Hopefully, as you see this part of the mind, you will want to become free of its menacing and destructive forces.

Why do we listen to a mind that berates, insults, and generally doesn't make us feel good? *We listen because we think that is who we are. We believe our very identity is the mind of unwanted thoughts.* Thoughts then become addictive, as the mind takes over, making us believe it is us, feeding us a frenzy of thoughts that circle with no solution, greatly disturbing and destroying a much-needed peace. We believe the only way to live is with the constant noise in our head, so we simply accept it as a way of life. We also believe that our past experiences, thoughts, and the emotions that arise from these thoughts make us who we are.

It may be hard to believe the endless, unwanted thoughts inside our head are the real and true cause of our anxious and stress-filled worries. The real and true cause of our anger and sadness. Thoughts *are* the real and true cause of all that makes you feel weighed down, depressed. The truth is, thoughts are also the true cause of our "problems"! Another truth is that *you are not your thoughts.* Once thoughts become unwanted thoughts, they are inconsequential and meaningless.

Fortunately, these unwanted thoughts coming from an entity that is an abuser and tormentor are really powerless and weak! When you restore your natural state of peace, harmony, and joy, as you are doing in the practices here, all thoughts, emotions, and feelings that weigh you down simply dissolve and disappear into nothingness!

THE FALSE SENSE OF SEPARATION

You came into this world simply alive and thriving.

How did you lose that?

More and more, you experienced yourself as separate and not connected. You began to identify with the past history and familiar habits of all those around you, and slowly but surely, you began to identify with your own past experiences, rehashing everything that "happened" to you. You also began to conform to the rigid expectations of society. A feeling of being separate in the world produced a sense of fear within, and with that fear came a new sense of trying to control everything and everyone. Along came yet another negative recognition: "me and mine."

A feeling of separateness and everything and everyone being "another" became a normal experience of life. Soon, competition and the need to win and the need to be right become essential.

As thoughts come through the separate, fearful mind, everything gets labeled and categorized. Nothing is accepted for its own unique and inherent beauty. Everything, to this mind, is only a name, never recognizing the profound depth of a tree, a flower, a person, or an animal. This naming, labeling, and categorizing further creates a sense of separation between you, everything, and everyone, causing conflict in relationships. When we think of someone or something as only a name, a member of a group, and separate, we miss the beauty within, producing a sense of judgment and criticism. This one is better, whereas this one is not so good. The judgmental, impatient mind hurries you along. If for a fleeting moment you want to capture the essence of nature's beauty, this mind will say to you, why waste time looking at a flower; you've no time for that!

As a separate self, a need for identity develops. If there is no identity, then who are we? The false mind creates "the story of me," which we become identified with as every thought is filtered through the experiences of our past history, the past history of those who raised us, our community, our school system, the culture and society we experienced growing up, and the society we are experiencing today.

This habitual way of experiencing life seeps through and flaws every thought, every emotion. We become limited in our ability to clearly see each event, each situation that confronts us. We interpret life through a fog, distorting the truth. Now a woman who experienced being abandoned by her father may have fear in her heart, and she may project that experience onto every man she meets.

The voice of unwanted thoughts coming from the false mind rehashes again and again our past and all the "bad" we experienced, energizing a solid identification with this voice and its thoughts that endlessly "talks" about the drama and problems, "hitting" us with emotions, further re-enforcing the belief that this mind is who we are. The voice is accepted as our self, as thoughts and their emotions are filled with the memory of our experience of past pain of anger, sadness, and regrets, as well as the tension, anxiety, and dread of a fearful, worrisome future.

The more we believe we are this false mind and the more we identify with it, the more it becomes obsessive and relentless, taking so much control, so much possession, that every feeling, every thought, and every emotion is taken in as if it is who we are—rather than the aware, Conscious presence.

When we believe we are this mind, it takes full control, producing thoughts that loop and circle around and around, filled with illusions of the past and the future. Illusions of the past are filled with self-narratives of primarily all the "bad" that happened. Illusions of the future contain imagined worst-case scenarios brimming with fear—and worry or anticipation of something, somehow, better in the future, despite all the chaos going on now.

Living in the pain of the past and the anticipation of the future is wasted time and wasted life. It is a life not lived. And this, as Eckhart Tolle wrote in *The Power of Now*, is the "core error… an illusion that we are nothing more than our mind and our physical body." Living this "core error" on a daily basis with the belief that we are no more than our thoughts, emotions, and our physical bodies has produced a mind filled with continuous, non-stop negative mental chatter.

Believing we are only our physical body and the mind limits our vision and image of who we really are—a being who lives in the moment, in the simplicity of peace, aware of their own power. The continuously noisy mind filled with turmoil prevents us from connecting with our peaceful True Self. It is vital to release the "noise" of useless thoughts so we can find our peaceful, serene truth. For it is in peace—and truth—that we open to the gifts in life.

The false mind produces a continuous stream of anger and fear, as well as an endless supply of emotional turmoil, which we categorize and label and give more attention to. The more totally identified we are with this fearful, angry mind, the more emotional pain we will have. An intense thought will produce a strong emotion, and a strong emotion will then produce an intense thought, generating a vicious cycle over and over again.

The false mind also produces an intense loss of energy and vitality, and yet, it seems to have become an accepted way of life. This out-of-control false mind causes emotional and physical pain the moment an intense thought produces a strong emotional energy charge. A trauma from the past remembered as a sad event, or a loss, generates a string of thoughts that quickly turn into emotional pain. As you think of the future with fear, the intense thought will also reflect somewhere in your body as a strong emotion. The strong energy charge produces "hurtful" emotional pain—in your stomach, your head, anywhere in your physical body. Both kinds of thoughts, whether from the past or from the future, are not real. They are both projections of this untruthful mind. To think of this mind as an *untruthful mental and physical abuser* is the truth. Another truth is that this mind is a tormentor and a bully that does not easily allow you to become free of its possessive, addictive, and destructive ways.

This false mind of darkness wants to make you believe that it can solve the emotional pain of a problem. However, it cannot because it *is* the problem. Every thought that produces emotional and physical pain and fear comes from this false mind. As an entity that wants to continue its existence, it holds you prisoner, wanting you to believe in it fully, totally, and unequivocally.

If something in your life did not turn out the way you would have liked, the mind rationalizes the situation for you, and you may feel better, but it is never lasting.

Let's say you remember a loss you suffered from the past. It could be a loss of money, a relationship, a job, or the loss of a loved one. You begin to feel regret and guilt about something you may have said or done, as a picture of that event unfolds in your mind's eye. You think you may have been wrong; perhaps you shouldn't have said or done something. All unwanted thoughts of the past are of a lower energy and come from this false mind. The thoughts of a "bad" experience in the past are so intense that they become strong energy charges of emotion. You are now fully immersed, involved, and feel weakened by the emotional pain the false mind of unwanted thoughts is giving you. *Remember that it is an untruthful physical abuser!*

This lower-energy false mind begins a mental dialogue with you, telling you to remember the "terrible" things done to you. It tells you that what you said or did was the "right" thing or maybe the "wrong" thing. The lower-energy mind never comes to the middle, the center of your Self. This false mind cannot enter your centered Self because its darkness consists of low energy, and it is not in alignment with your higher-energy, powerful light.

This untruthful false mind capriciously wants to keep you involved in thoughts of the past or of the future because, when you are present and aware at this moment, you do not need thoughts. However, this mind *does* need thoughts to survive and will lose its life without your "thinking mind."

You do not need to experience the detrimental effects of emotional pain coming from a painful past or emotional pain coming from fear of the future.

It is important to remember that past and future thoughts are primarily unwanted thoughts that make you suffer. Protect yourself by coming into the safe shelter of your center: calm yourself with your breath, become aware of your surroundings in the now moment, and sense your inner energetic life force, life streaming through the powerful You. The more that you come to your calm and peaceful center, the easier it will be to become your True Self, an enlightened being, your Self in Consciousness.

BECOME FREE. DO IT AS IF YOUR LIFE DEPENDS ON IT... BECAUSE IT DOES!

To become free of a painful past and a worrisome future, you do not need to analyze and examine why an emotional pain is making you suffer. As you practice simply being consciously aware moment to moment, you are free of the pollution coming from the mind of unwanted thoughts. The "heart of yourself" is a safe and secure place.

You have ease and comfort in Consciousness, where the pain from the past and worry about what the future holds simply vanishes. As you put your attention on yourself within, your mental, emotional, and physical self are now free of the heavy weight of depressive thoughts.

In the heart of your Self, where it is pure and simple, you do not believe something is good or bad, right or wrong; you are simply being. In the middle, centered, heart of your Self, you are aware of life within and all around you, seeing only the best of life in a very neutral space. You never worry about having to be right or the best at anything. Nor do you yearn, long, maneuver, or scheme to try to get things to work out in your favor.

However, you are now more powerful than ever because rather than having useless, mindless noise within that is producing anger and fear, you have free space, giving more depth to the peace you feel, more depth to the compassion and love you feel, and more depth to the joy you feel. You have made room for so much more to come into your life. Life now becomes easier and gentler, taking shape and form without you having to try to do or make an effort to control anything. Sometimes making you feel as if the things you used to try to control now just "fall into place," making life easier. It is simple and pure right in the centered, heart of your Self.

Through a more spacious mind, you will now receive insights and inspiration about something you want to create that you feel will bring success in the future, a goal you may have.

FREEDOM IS AS CLOSE
AS YOUR FINGERTIPS

If, in the course of your day, you are finding it difficult to distance yourself from unwanted thoughts, emotions, and feelings, freedom is as close as your fingertips. Do the following when you feel overwhelmed with unwanted thoughts:

Raise your hand and look at it. With no judgment of your hand, simply feel the life force energy flowing through it. As you do, thoughts cease instantly because your attention has shifted to yourself within. Continue by expanding your awareness into your inner Self, from your head to your toes. As you include awareness of yourself, unwanted thoughts are kept at a distance, further relieving your mental, emotional, and physical body of emotional pain. In this state of awareness, you are in a powerful, inner sanctuary of freedom.

As you align with a powerful life force energy by living in awareness, moment to moment, you become open to receiving more of what you are consciously aware of and, therefore, accepting that into your life. For when you are aware and in acceptance of life in whatever way it presents itself, you are appreciating life. Appreciation has a very high-vibrational energetic force. You *will* attract and reflect back into your life whatever energy goes through your mind. You do not want any kind of lower energy that will reflect back into your life the same lower energy through situations and circumstances. Stay positive, energized, and invigorated for life! Always finding the best in life, in whole-hearted acceptance and appreciation.

To counteract and offset the endless thoughts that bring you down, zapping your energetic life force, repeat "That's not true!" often throughout the day. It's a good way to remember the detrimental effects that negative thoughts and emotions transport and cause, and a good way to transition to uplifting, better-energy thoughts and emotions that will translate into better experiences naturally unfolding in your life.

Keep your mind positive and uplifted throughout your day. Make it a point to notice everything that surrounds you in each moment, whether it is nature or the inherent beauty in your surroundings, without names or labels. Whatever you look at, take it in with all your senses. Make it a habit to use your five senses, and the world will change and become more alive. Notice the light, the patterns, the textures, the sounds, and the scents. The mind is still and quiet as you give attention and awareness to whatever surrounds you daily. Create a habit of finding only the good and the best of life. Be deliberate and purposeful as you look around and see only what raises and boosts your mood—thereby raising your energetic field. You, as a conscious presence, are never in a lower-energy mood. It is not you!

There is much to be gained as you are uplifted and positive. You are in full control, no longer enslaved by an out-of-control mind. You are creating space in between thoughts, gaining the light of Consciousness. You are relieved of lower-energy thoughts, improving your health at that moment.

Paying attention and being aware of your Self, a powerful being, contains a profound depth that the false ego-mind does not know. It knows nothing of the miracle of your breath, nothing of the energetic life force flowing through you, and nothing of the infinite cosmic connection of which you are a part.

You will soon realize that it is far better—and easier—to quiet and cease unwanted thoughts than to continue on the perilous path of the possible destruction of your mental and physical health—and your life!

There *is* a painless way to free yourself from thoughts that hurt and harm. True tragedy would be to continue on this perilous path, believing you are nothing more than the small, inconsequential false mind.

PRACTICES AND SUMMARY
OF CHAPTER SEVEN

YOU ARE NOT YOUR THOUGHTS

Practice: Raise your hand and look at it to release overwhelming thoughts

Do the following when you are overwhelmed with unwanted thoughts:

1. Raise your hand and look at it. With no judgment of your hand, simply feel the life force energy flowing through it. As you do, thoughts cease instantly because your attention has shifted to yourself within. Continue by expanding your awareness into your inner Self, from your head to your toes. As you include awareness of yourself within, unwanted thoughts are kept at a distance, relieving your mental, emotional, and physical body.

2. Counter unwanted thoughts that come from a false mind by saying "That's not true" often during the day. It is a good time to remember to *be* in a positive, uplifting energy. Also, it's a good time to remember you have a choice between feeling good or bad.

3. Live as your centered, breathing, aware Self. It is a safe haven, a secure place where you feel more depth of peace, more depth of joy. You, as a conscious presence, are never in a lower mood. It is not you!

SUMMARY

1. It is vital to consider the false ego-mind as a demeaning and cruel perpetrator, a tormentor that berates, belittles, and abuses. Only then will we be convinced of its menacing force in a world that accepts its destructive tendencies.

2. Why do we listen to a mind that berates, insults, and generally doesn't make us feel good? We listen because we believe it is who we are. We believe our identity is the false mind of unwanted thoughts. We also believe the constant noise in our head is just a normal part of life.

3. Thoughts that come from the false mind are the real and true cause of all that makes you feel weighed down, depressed, and just plain bad. These unwanted thoughts are also the cause of all of your "problems."

4. You do not need thoughts when you are peaceful and joyous.

5. Fortunately, these unwanted thoughts are insubstantial, inconsequential, and weak. You can dissolve them through your powerful light, freeing you for good.

6. As we grew from infancy, our natural sense of aliveness and awe, without judgment, turned into a feeling of being separate and not connected. Fear developed, and with it, a need to control everything and everyone. Through this fear, the false mind was developed.

7. We begin to identify with the false mind that promotes the "story of me." And we begin to believe this false, noisy mind that produces past pain and future worry, "hitting" us with emotional pain.

8. Our "core error" is believing we are nothing more than our noisy mind and our physical bodies. The noisy mind keeps us from experiencing our natural peace, joy, and aliveness.

9. Remember that the false mind is an untruthful physical abuser! It wants you to hold on to intense, emotional thoughts because without your thinking mind, it will lose its life.

Chapter Eight

THE OBSERVER

*To become an "observer" is to open the
doorway of Consciousness and step inside
the vast space that creates worlds*

A s an observer, you stand at the welcoming door of your
Self in Consciousness—the vast and limitless power that
is You. You are balanced and in harmony in the ever-widening
and expanding path of Consciousness.

This "knowing" realization is a turning point and opens up
what Eckhart Tolle describes as "a new activation of
Consciousness."

Becoming calm and at peace simply observing thoughts means
you have come to a *realization*—not a thought—of who you
really are, an aware observer of life as it unfolds into situations,
circumstances, and events. You now realize that you are not

the identity you thought, of your past experiences or your judgmental likes and dislikes. You are not just your outer physical shell or your mind of fearful and anger-driven thoughts. And you are not the one that analyzes and interprets each and every event and situation that unfolds in life. The realization comes as you experience your conscious presence over here while the mind of unwanted thoughts is over there being observed by you.

This realization of yourself as a peaceful observer solidly transitions into being the True You in your daily life. You have created the space that is needed when something doesn't happen in quite the way you would like. You can now detach and not react. As you practice simply being an observer of thoughts, anchored in your stillness within, you gain a more resilient nature, able to respond differently to a situation. When something "goes wrong," you can now observe it without judgment nor involvement and easily come back to your vantage point of observing unwanted thoughts and situations in calmness.

Becoming an observer of your thoughts is not *doing*, but *being*. *As an observer of thoughts, you experience* who you were born to *be,* a peaceful Self in Consciousness, with no involvement, no interpretation, no judgment. While it may appear to be a passive state, it is really a powerfully potent way to live life.

Observe a thought you do not want without cynicism, criticism, nor condemnation. As you do, you create distance and detachment from a false mind that all too often destroys lives and can easily destroy yours through dis-ease, disillusionment, or "unhappiness." As you observe the wandering mind and come back again and again to awareness of your Self, you will gain, in those moments, relief from mental and emotional pain. You will also, in that same moment, protect your physical self from harm. Eventually, the practice of observing, watching, and being a witness to thoughts will transition to simply "being."

OBSERVING THOUGHTS
IS FINDING THE TRUE YOU

As you *feel* your high-energy Self in Consciousness, you *know* you are not your mind of unwanted thoughts and emotions that cause misery and suffering. You *know* you are not just a physical body, the "shell" of your physical self. This *knowing* is not a thought, but a new experience of your aware Self as a conscious presence. As you observe thoughts that are filled with anger, anxiety, and fear at a distance, without involvement or indulgence, you realize you are the far-removed peaceful and aware observer and, therefore, not one and the same with the false mind of unwanted thoughts. Remaining the peaceful observer and now free of unwanted thinking is testament and proof that you were never the mind of hurtful and upsetting unwanted thoughts, nor were you only the physical outer shell you thought of as yourself.

You can now explore and become acquainted with a vast inner Self that will now make life much easier to live. You have freed yourself from the weight of depressed thoughts. You have set yourself free from the jail cell of negative emotions.

Becoming free of a lifetime of being imprisoned with lower-energy thinking that once depleted you mentally and physically puts you on the path to living life in its most exhilarating state, at one with it, and more able than ever to find beauty in simply *being*. Through the absence of the negative mental chatter that once caused you so much upheaval and emotional pain, your natural qualities can come to the surface: compassion and loving kindness, cooperation and connectedness, peace and joy.

These qualities come from a dimension of more depth and stability. You do not have to work hard to acquire these qualities; they are already a natural part of You as you gain Consciousness, and you *will feel* them. The moment you feel compassion, you will know that you are, at that moment, a conscious being—a *presence*.

As a conscious being, you are kind, compassionate, and *very powerful*. These qualities are what will help you be a better observer of thoughts. For once you are consciously aware—of your breath, your inner being, and your surroundings—you are no longer judgmental, cynical, or critical, nor do you feel resentment nor malice toward others. You are more allowing than ever, not trying to push anything for your benefit. You are no longer reacting to what someone said or to how a situation did not turn out the way you would have liked. You are now a powerful being, in more control than ever because the insignificant, unimportant things do not take up room in your life. You are no longer reactive to a burned dinner, a misbehaving child, or someone's rude remarks. With more spaciousness in your mind, you now respond more wisely, you know what to do, and you now realize that a challenge has within it a high potential for growth.

As you become these qualities, *you* become the director of your life, not the false mind pretending to be you, generating chaos and malice. You can now, more easily than ever, observe and notice an unwanted thought in non-judgment that will easily dissolve.

As peaceful observers of thoughts in non-judgment, we stop controlling thoughts, and thoughts stop controlling us. Pushing away or trying to get rid of a thought will only make that thought come back again and again. We are simply being allowing and accepting as we observe a thought coming through our space.

HOW DO I OBSERVE A THOUGHT?

If you are having difficulty observing thoughts, the following will give you an idea of how unwanted thoughts can be treated:

Imagine you are sitting on a park bench, immersed in the awareness of your Self and your surroundings. You're taking in the beauty and essence of a tree in non-thought (your conscious presence), its leaves falling with streams of sunlight reflecting on the grass. On your right, you become aware that someone (a thought) is about to walk in front of you. As the person (thought) passes in front of you, you observe with no involvement, no judgment. The person simply passes through your space. You do not know where they came from nor where they are going, and that's okay. You do not categorize, label, or judge. You easily come back to the changing patterns of sunlight on the grass and the flowing leaves falling from the tree, representing the awareness of your conscious presence—your breath and your inner energetic field.

This is you in Consciousness, aware of changing and shifting patterns within and all that surrounds you in the outside world. Observe thoughts as they pass with no involvement and no judgment, easily and effortlessly, in simple awareness of your calm inner being and your surroundings.

You can be consciously aware in your kitchen, in your living room, or in front of a blank wall. You will feel your inner peaceful Self, vibrant and alive, anywhere you happen to be. You will feel your alive presence more and more as you practice coming back to your aware Self again and again. You are protecting your pure, calm inner Self as you observe, watch, and witness unwanted thoughts. As you practice observing thoughts, you are also practicing detaching from challenging situations that unfold in life.

If you find it challenging to observe unwanted thoughts as you go about your day, be imaginative, creative, and playful in creating ways to dissolve them. You might imagine unwanted thoughts as balloons floating toward the sky as you brush them away lightly with a feather. Or you may simply say "thinking" as a thought passes through, thereby acknowledging but not getting involved in the thought. To further help yourself stop resisting and "trying to get rid of" a thought, imagine a clear blue sky. As an unwanted thought comes through, imagine a white puffy cloud passing through the sky, dissolving and disappearing. You are the vast blue sky behind the stormy clouds that gather and obscure the vast beauty that is really who you are.

While thoughts may continue to make their way through, you are now *more aware*. With practice, you will become more and more free, observing low-energy thoughts from afar, protecting your inner space from the debris and pollution of thoughts that de-energize and zap your vitality. Observing thoughts in non-judgment will translate into everyday situations, which you will now simply notice in non-reaction. Eventually, you will naturally be consciously aware, taking in life all around you in total awareness, no longer needing to be a guard of your space.

THE POWER OF OBSERVING

The energy of observing thoughts is powerful because thoughts are no longer being energized through your total immersion and involvement in them. There is also a high-powered energy now shifted to You, at peace in pure conscious presence. Observing is awareness with no judgment, and awareness is who you really are.

When you become aware of an unwanted thought, observe it, and if it contains an emotion, feel the energy of the emotion fully. You are not getting involved in its content, just the *feeling* of the energy. Energy, whether good or "bad," is energy nonetheless and can be used in a beneficial way. *"Feel" the "bad" energy, imagining yourself transparent—just as you practiced in preceding chapters—as it passes through you. Once it passes through you, it becomes light. You have dissolved and turned into light, without malice or judgment, an energy that might have caused you great harm.*

Go into it fully, feeling it, in non-thought and non-indulgence. While it may seem frightening to face an emotional pain, the painful emotion coming from the darkness of a thought is really meaningless and insubstantial in relation to the power of your Self in the light—the higher energy of awareness, your Self in Consciousness.

If you experience the mind of unwanted thoughts re-emerging, it comes from the false self that wants to hold on and wants to make it seem complicated to let go. Your True Self is serene and at peace, able to let go easily. Becoming aware of a thought of a lower energy is a celebration in itself. Once you become aware of an unwanted thought, you *are* conscious presence, and you *are* your True Self at the moment you become aware!

How do you feel at this moment? Use how you feel as an indicator, letting you know whether you are in a high energy or a low energy. Catch moments in which you feel moody, irritated, or weighed down in depressive thoughts quickly, so you can shift your attention to the higher energy of a good feeling.

The *feelings* that are of a lower energy are actually like a good friend that alerts you. The feelings of anger, guilt, and sadness, or anxiety, stress, and fear, or any low-energy feeling are like a warning alarm, alerting you to come back, again, to a good feeling. Use your breath as a calming tool, and observe the thought or emotion with no indulgence. You may use any of the calming "tools" you have practiced, such as becoming transparent, affirming a statement such as "That's not true!" or sounding your note.

Unwanted thoughts *will* dissolve through your powerful observation and through your lack of attention on the content of the thoughts.

The razor-sharp "tool" of standing in observation has been used to transform an outside world's undesirable situation:

Gandhi is respected and revered almost a century later as a great leader who freed India from English dominance. Instead of using weapons, malice, or war, he put together a powerful force of citizens simply standing up in non-violent "aware observance." Through a multitude of events, in the end it was this powerful non-violent act of a unified citizenry standing as "the witnessing watchers and observers" that achieved the retreat of English forces, freeing India.

You are doing the same thing as you hold unwanted thoughts, emotions, and feelings in aware observance. Science understands the energy interaction between object and subject, how both the object and subject change through observation. A divided, disorderly mind cannot change anything; only a mind whole and complete, anchored in the present moment, can observe and make a difference. You will learn more about the power of the present moment in the next chapter.

You have now become aware of how unwanted thoughts coming from a past emotional pain or the worry of a "made-up" future is causing difficulty in your life, leading to an experience of life as "not easy." As you observe thoughts in the purity of your Self in Consciousness, you have opened to freedom from anguish, anger, pain, and fear. A new connection to a powerful force is now yours, rewarding you with a better life.

THE OBSERVER

Practice: Observing unwanted thoughts

If you are having difficulty observing thoughts, the following will give you an idea of how unwanted thoughts can be observed:

1. Imagine you are sitting on a park bench, immersed in the beauty and essence of a tree in non-thought (your conscious awareness). Its leaves are falling, and streams of sunlight reflect on the grass. On your right, you become aware that someone (a thought) is about to walk in front of you. As the person passes in front of you, you observe with no involvement, no judgment. The person simply passes through your space. You do not know where they came from nor where they are going, and that's okay. You do not categorize, label, or judge. You easily come back to the changing patterns of sunlight on the grass and the flowing leaves falling from the tree, representing the awareness of your conscious presence—your breath and your inner energetic field.

2. Appreciate feelings because feelings are like a good friend, an indicator, alerting you of lower-energy thoughts that weigh you down, producing a moody, irritating, or sad emotion. Stop often throughout the day to take note of how you feel.

SUMMARY

1. To become an observer and watcher of thoughts is to celebrate a "new activation of Consciousness," a path to your True Self, who you really are. You are not the fear-driven, anxious human being you think of as yourself.

2. A realization of who you really are is not a thought. You realize you are your True Self, a *presence,* here watching a thought that is over there, at a distance. You realize you are an observer of thoughts. You are not your thoughts.

3. As a peaceful observer of unwanted thoughts, you can now detach and not react. You become resilient in your daily life because you have practiced coming back easily to the vantage point of your True Self again and again.

4. As an observer, you are not "doing" but "being." You are simply "being" in a safe, calm, and soothing place. It is an experience of yourself without judgment, interpretation, nor involvement.

5. As a peaceful observer, you can now explore the vast inner space that is *you*. You are free to explore the wonder and beauty of life. Freer than ever, you can live life in its most exhilarating and stimulating way!

6. Now freed of unwanted thoughts that weigh you down, your natural qualities of love and compassion, inner peace, and joy become more evident.

7. You are now more in control than ever, not reacting to what someone says or does. You are the director of your life, aware of a vast inner space, no longer immersed in struggle and conflict.

8. The power of observance rests in the interaction between object and subject as both change through the energy of observation. However, you may use the many doorways you have learned here: awareness of yourself within, affirmations, mantras, sounding your unique note, and making yourself transparent, among others.

9. The power of observance has opened the door to a vast and unlimited connection. It is now possible to create unlimited possibilities in life.

Chapter Nine

THE PRESENT MOMENT, NOW

*The present moment is the gift of life
and is the only place life truly exists*

The present moment—now—is the gift of life, for the only place life truly exists and can truly be lived is in this moment. To thrive in life is to live in the splendor and fascination of this moment, just as you did when you came into this world. The present moment cannot be complete, however, until you become the *awareness* that is who you really are.

Your aware presence in this moment *can never* be dissolved, broken up, or made to disappear. It is a powerful light. Yet unwanted thoughts *can* be de-energized, weakened, and dissolved altogether as you shine your powerful light of awareness on them. Imagine the sun's rays, powerful and strong, uncovering with its light every crevice, valley, and break in the landscape. With the darkness dissolved, there is now a clear landscape. As you imagine your powerful light within easily dissolving the darkness of feelings, thoughts, and emotions, your clear True Self, your *presence,* will emerge.

These unwanted thoughts, feelings, and emotions have nothing to do with expansion and growth, and do not come from truth. Your *aware* attention of *yourself and your surroundings* in the timeless now is safe, secure, powerful—and <u>true</u>. When you are present and aware at this moment in the truth of your centered Self, unwanted and untruthful thoughts that depress and weigh you down cannot enter.

Can you *feel* your inner life force energy *now?*

It takes practice, but there is much to be gained. As you give *aware* attention to your life force energy streaming through you *now,* you are tapping into pure Consciousness. For awareness of yourself within, as well as what surrounds you, *is* Consciousness that is awakening and connecting you to an infinite, vast, and eternal space. You are actually accelerating your path to Consciousness. At the same time, your *presence,* now free of mental commotion, can improve your mental and physical health and well-being.

Practice: Feeling and gaining aware presence

Do the following so you can practice "feeling" aware *presence*: Inhale and exhale deeply until you feel calm. Relax every muscle in your body, the muscles in your face, arms, chest, stomach, legs, and feet. Inhale as you imagine a luminous light all around you. Exhale this light into your inner Self in awareness of life streaming through your blood vessels, the atoms and molecules in your cells, and your unique DNA right in the middle of each cell. Keep inhaling and exhaling and flooding every "nook and cranny" of your inner body with light. Let go of any mental pictures and "feel" your life force energy. Practice often so that you can feel your inner energy field moment to moment. Eventually, you will simply *be* aware *presence* without effort.

Eckhart Tolle wrote that our body and cells love the attention we give to them.

Practice: Improving your immune system

Your powerful aware presence can now influence the health of your immune system:

Take three or four flowing, easy breaths, or as many as you need until you feel calm. Inhale, and as you exhale, imagine light permeating throughout your body from your head to your toes, invigorating and rejuvenating the health of your cells.

Expand radiant, brilliant light throughout your body in a blissful, aware state, as each cell takes in the energy and attention that is imagined by a powerful you at this moment. Continue for as long as you like. This practice will become more powerful as you gain an aware presence.

Through the powerful awareness and feeling energy of your presence, your life will change. You will let go for good of emotional pain and worry. Presence is the key that will "touch" the rich space that leads to a better life. You will feel lighter in spirit, soaring high in new vitality and enthusiasm.

MOVE FORWARD BUT
ALLOW FOR SETBACKS

Living in the present moment does not mean, however, you will no longer have situations or obstacles that you interpret as troublesome. You will have moments when someone or something will get in the way to make it difficult to accomplish what you would like. You may completely "lose it." If you don't quite find presence in a situation, don't be hard on yourself; it's natural to lose presence, as long as you can quickly come back to your aware Self at this moment. Remember that as soon as you become aware that your mind has wandered off into negativity, you *are* consciously aware and in Consciousness at that moment! It is always more important to come back quickly to being present than to try being present in each moment.

When you have presence, you respond differently to a situation, without malice, without anger, and without judgment. Your presence, at the moment you experience a situation, will determine and give fuel to a difficult situation's outcome. You will either find a way to go around it or transform it, utilizing a mind that is more spacious, clear, and present, freer of clutter and disorder.

Eventually, your presence will be second nature, effortless. The good news is that you can be present as quickly as this very moment. The present moment never separates itself from you; it is always there for you, available *now*. Never worry that you are not "getting it." To do so is to revert back to the small, false mind. You can, in each moment, start over and be your conscious Self as quickly as now!

When something "goes wrong," you need to be present in non-reaction. Once you react, your presence is lost. Take a few deep breaths, and *feel your conscious presence* in this moment. Practice awareness of your inner life force and simply "be" *presence* in peace and calm within. You will reinforce a stable foundation, like a flowing tree with deep roots. Nothing that "goes wrong" can overrule and dominate the powerful depth and alignment of your presence. Soon, with persistent practice of *presence* in the moment, a powerful depth of alignment with source energy will make life "work" better. You become empowered, and life changes in positive ways.

Be consciously present not only when obstacles and blocks in daily life are challenging, but also in the most calm, ordinary, and mundane situations. Your persistent practice will pay off, creating better life experiences, as well as better relationships, much of it having to do with your now peaceful acceptance rather than reaction to life in the moment. Your fragmented, broken, and divisive "false, small mind" that reflected back more of the same low energy is no longer there to jeopardize every situation. Ultimately, with more inner peace and serenity, a relationship can flourish and succeed. When you feel good, you attract more of the same into your life. Whatever you feel within, whether peace, harmony, and ease, or stress, anxiety, and fear, will reflect back as events and situations that match your either high or low energy. Your awareness in the present moment is crucial. Become the protector and guard of your Self within!

Remember to stop during your day to feel your mood. A depressed and weighed-down feeling is not you. You are a consciously aware, peaceful being!

You have been reminded here again and again of all the good and great that is in store for you as you practice being your Self in Consciousness and having in-the-moment awareness. You have realized the importance of living only in the simplicity of now, "allowing" everything to be just as it is without yearning nor trying to change anything. Remember that what you are "allowing" is the present moment, not a situation you must change. Any situation that weighs you down is a situation that must be changed. However, you will now have the clear mind of *presence* to change it with much less struggle and more ease.

Living in the moment also means not *anticipating* a time in the future that you believe will be more exciting. Living in *anticipation* of a moment in the future is not living your life now. Savor and bask in the magic of your life-giving breath and your five senses. Watch an early morning sunrise or an evening sunset, the light's dazzling spectrum of colors. With an awareness of your breath and inner Self, be aware of the subtle joy, the peace, the freedom. Watch as the brilliance of the sunrise easily blankets the darkness in light, without strife, without battle, or as the vibrant sun easily allows the darkness. The sun's light will come back again and again, gentle, loyal, and committed. To watch nature is to be in awe and to learn from it.

We have a tendency to think of the present moment as only a stepping stone to a more important moment, either short or long term: cooking dinner and *rushing* through a meal before a movie, *looking forward to* and anticipating a wedding or any future event, looking *forward* to retirement. Living in this way means we never really live life to its fullest, never actually live life in the only place our life exists—now!

HOW DO I STAY PRESENT WITHOUT THE MIND TAKING OVER?

The present moment is stable, reliable, unwavering, and committed, always available. You do not have to try or put forth effort to be here. Calm yourself through your breath. Once we breathe deeply, it is as if there is now an open space, felt by the heart, of increasing peace.

The present moment, a profound and unlimited space, is timeless. As you are at peace and aware, observe the natural world around you. Can you tell what time it is? Does it really matter? Our daily lives are extremely time-oriented. When you must be some place at a certain time, *be* there in *presence*, aware and alert, and in observance of everything before you. You can now get more done in a faster time frame because the noisy, commotion-filled mind is no longer there, which will also give you more focus and better concentration. And, of course, new ideas and insights will come into your more spacious mind, helping you to be more productive as you work in a time-oriented world.

"Happiness" comes from the dualistic patterns of the world we live in and only relies on whatever "happens" to you in your daily life. The dualistic mind pattern is happy and then sad, finding pleasure and then dis-pleasure. Notice how an outside world's pattern of extremes, of one way then another, is short-lived. There always seems to be a high-energy beginning—happiness—and a low energetic end—sadness. Notice how addictive behaviors that we find pleasurable, like food or shopping, eventually end in the consequences of being overweight or facing mounting bills. Have you ever noticed how "happiness" can be so elusive, happening and then leaving very quickly? Everything changes and never has a stable foundation in our worldly experience. Relationships change. Careers change. There might be instances when happiness will stay for a longer time period; however, sooner or later, something will change or diminish the happiness that we once felt.

When you live more and more in the purity of Consciousness in this moment, what you once experienced as "happiness" will turn into joy, a *feeling* coming from a place of more profound depth and wisdom. You will feel joy when you least expect it because joy does not rely on what happens in an outside world. You may be doing something mundane and unexciting like a chore, and you will feel joy. It will come through naturally with no effort on your part. Since you are now free of troublesome thoughts and emotions, free of a relentless, problem-seeking mind that once drove you crazy, you now have more good reasons than ever for joy! And there is more! For once you feel joy for no reason at all, you know you are living from a vast, unlimited space where you can now open to unlimited possibilities in your life. You now have unlimited potential that can come about through what you do, think, and say.

As we live more and more present and aware, a pattern emerges, like a beautiful tapestry that connects people and situations perfectly. Events seem to magically unfold. You are at the right place at the right time; you meet the right person that can help you with your goal. You become aligned with an intelligent creative force that brings about synchronicities.

SMALL, BUT SIGNIFICANT MIRACLES

A synchronistic event occurred to Samantha, who lives aware of the moment and practices Consciousness on a daily basis.

Samantha owns a business with two fifteen-passenger buses and, realizing that her business is expanding, she thought about and envisioned adding a bigger passenger bus. However, after pricing bigger buses, she realized she had to wait before one could be purchased. Not giving it any more thought, days later, in a conversation with her mechanic, he told her that he had recently been given a twenty-five-passenger bus, and he would be willing to sell it to her for an outrageously small price of one thousand dollars! She invested another small amount for mechanical fixtures, and she now has a good-working bigger bus! She was able to accomplish this easily and with no struggle!

Samantha enjoys sharing her synchronistic experiences that unfold often and effortlessly in her life. An energy of joyous expectancy, as well as her expanding Consciousness, seems to attract more of the same to "magically" unfold in her life. The attitude of joyous expectancy is many times more powerful than one of anxiety and stress.

Through Consciousness, we increasingly become a part of a creative, intelligent force that can help us put together business deals, help us find the perfect office, just as we envisioned it, or lead us to the right size and color shirt. Every synchronicity that happens through this all-knowing creation seems to happen for the good of all concerned.

Danielle is also someone who maintains a purposeful awareness of the present moment, understanding that the present moment is the only place life truly exists. Through a nurtured awareness, she has developed an appreciation of nature; the exuberant formation of clouds that bring rain, the rolling hills that she sees from her kitchen. Through practice, she is, more easily than ever, finding the bliss of the present moment in non-thought, through her love of music in aware, relaxed moments. A blissful state is the essence of meditation.

By living life in each powerful moment with an increasing emergence of high-energy feelings like joy and peace, life now works for you, not against you! Immersed in the present moment, you no longer rely on an outside world to bring you "happiness." With lower energies of conflict and strife gone, you attract the higher energy of *presence*. Can you see how we do, indeed, create our own life? Joyous, uplifting excitement and calm inner peace are reflected back into life, manifesting as harmonious and flowing situations.

When we connect to an infinite source energy in peace and acceptance, we no longer yearn, nor try to convince or manipulate someone so that we can have what we want. We are helped in ways we cannot really understand, and we do not need to understand. We need only to realize and become aware that help to live a life of ease is available. Simply living in alignment with a powerful flow of inner peace and awareness now, no longer immersed in worry or anxiety, is enough. We can then tap into the true bliss and the true "magic" of Consciousness at this moment.

We can also help events and situations to come about by writing goals or simply by thinking about goals consciously aware and fully present at the moment. Keep expanding on goals in a limitless way. Your imagination is a very powerful force. There is no harm in envisioning your dream life to its highest degree, without limits. However, as you envision, let it go; do not wonder how long it will take or if it will happen; simply stay present, neither wanting nor craving anything. Most importantly, become aware of doubt coming into your space, which hinders and blocks all higher energy! Today, it is about what you love to do, your purpose, and the creation of your entire life, no longer about the materialization of a single object and form. You, yourself, *are* a limitless space within; you do not need to imagine a future in scarcity and lack!

When you live within the concentrated energy of Consciousness—an awareness of your Self in the present moment in non-thought and non-judgment, you now bring something you want into your life through inspiration and creative ideas from a higher part of your mind. You will be "working," not from the outside in by busily "doing" and working hard first, but from the inside out, within the silence and awareness of your breath as you imagine the best outcome before you begin to work on your goal. Inspirational ideas and insights will now come from your spacious mind to help you accomplish your goal. These inspirational ideas and revelations will come to you more and more easily as you gain Consciousness, and you will no longer consider what you do as "work."

The limited, linear mind is what Einstein referred to as he said, "Knowledge is limited... imagination encircles the world." Einstein knew everything to be energy, and it is this more vast and unlimited energy that can be used as we focus our powerful attention and awareness on whatever we intend in this moment. Now we are open to a vaster expansion of knowledge through intuition, inspiration, and creative ideas, not just the knowledge we have gained in the span of a lifetime.

Living in the present moment, fully aware, especially of your life force energies within, has freed you and helped you let go of mental commotion and frenzied thoughts. The mind is now helpful, aware, and alert. You now have more space to think in clear, creative ways.

With the mind of problems no longer there, you emanate a new radiance and energy, a new excitement and aliveness. You are like a drop in a vast ocean, with the power of the whole. Your "space" within is ever-widening and growing, reflecting back into your life unlimited possibilities.

THE PRESENT MOMENT—NOW

1. Practice: Feeling and gaining presence

Do the following to practice *feeling* your life force energy within
so that you can gain *aware presence*:

Inhale and exhale deeply until you feel calm. Relax every
muscle in your body, the muscles in your face, arms, hands,
chest, stomach, legs, and feet. Inhale as you imagine a luminous
light all around you. Exhale this light into the life force energy
streaming through your blood vessels, the atoms and
molecules in your cells, your unique DNA right in the middle
of each cell. Keep inhaling and exhaling, flooding every "nook
and cranny" of your inner body with light. Let go of any mental
pictures, and *feel* your life force energy. Practice often so that
you can *feel* your inner energetic field moment to moment.
Eventually, you will simply be *presence* without effort.

2. Practice: Improving your immune system

As you live in *presence* moment to moment, you can influence
your immune system:

Inhale, and as you exhale, imagine light permeating throughout your body, from your head to your toes, invigorating and rejuvenating your cells. Expand radiant, brilliant light throughout your body in a blissful, aware state as each cell takes in the energy that is intended and imagined by a powerful you at this moment. Continue for as long as you like.

3. Strive for a higher energy moment to moment. Practice inner peace and an awareness of your increasing light through the doorway of your breath.

4. Savor and bask in the magic of your life-giving breath and your five senses.

5. Awareness is who you really are. Practice living in the awareness of your Self within—your presence at this moment. *Feeling presence* is the key that will help you dwell in your powerful inner space, bringing forth life's gifts and rewards.

6. As you feel the energy of your inner life force moment to moment, you *are presence* and you *are* in Consciousness. You will accelerate your path and change your life!

7. Don't be hard on yourself if you cannot find presence in a situation. It is more important to come back quickly than to try to be present in every moment. The moment you realize *you are not* consciously aware, you *are* consciously aware and present in that moment.

8. Take a couple of deep breaths, or as many as you need, to calm yourself when you feel angry, stressed, or anxious. Nothing that "goes wrong" can overrule or dominate your powerful depth of *presence,* which can be accessed *now* through the doorway of your breath.

SUMMARY

1. The present moment is the only place life exists. The past happened in its own moment, and the future will happen in its own moment also.

2. Your presence at the moment is a high energy that can actually change your life through having less struggle and more ease.

3. We have a tendency to think of the present moment as only a stepping stone to a more important moment—looking forward to a wedding or retirement. Living in this way means we never really live life to its fullest.

4. While "happiness" is short-lived and dependent on what happens in an outside world, joy comes when you least expect it, arising from the profound depth of your conscious presence. As you gain Consciousness, there is no end to the joy you can feel.

5. Envision your dream life in unlimited ways. As you connect with an infinite, abundant space, more and more, you will be open to limitless possibilities. Plan your future without limiting what you can have, be, or do. Be present and use your imagination!

Chapter Ten

SURRENDERING

Surrendering is trusting the natural flow of life

Imagine sitting on a sandy beach watching the seagulls glide, contemplating in awe a surf-rider's smooth moves on the waves, neither pushing nor resisting; the pounding waves break, and, mesmerized, you reflect on the ebb and flow of a giving and receiving sea.

As you watch, you become part of life's flow of currents, movements, and waves. You become one with the flow of life all around you; you breathe deeper, with your body more relaxed, in total awareness of the feel of grainy sand on your toes, the shimmering water, the exhilarating sounds, scents, and tastes. It is a simple moment in surrendered peace, aligned, and a match with a natural universal flow. You have freed your mind, body, and soul from a challenging world.

Throughout the practices here, you have practiced *presence,* awareness in peaceful calm. When you are at peace and calm and in full acceptance of whatever is before you as it occurs in the moment, not judging, fighting, or battling with it, you are in a surrendered state! Surrendering is not a decision we make in our head, a "willpower" that involves effort. Surrendering is peace from our head to our toes, no longer held in captivity of the false mind of thoughts that are judgmentally "trying" to control every circumstance, every event, and situation in life.

Imagine the serene and beautiful ocean scene suddenly not in alignment with the natural flows. What would happen if the seagull resisted the currents; would its controlled efforts look as graceful? Would flight be possible? Would the surf-rider's fluid moves look as supple, smooth, and elegant if he resisted the waves? Would there not be something wrong if the ocean suddenly stopped its natural ebb and flow? Whatever is not in alignment with the natural flows causes hardship, difficulty, and suffering in the world.

Would the dancer and the skater's attractively smooth flows still be possible if every move was thought about and controlled? Would the sounds of notes and lyrics be as beautiful if the musician and the singer resisted? The artist's brushstroke, the poet's pen? The world would be devoid of much beauty if everything was controlled through an anxious and stressed mind.

All around us, every day, in many more ways than we realize, are the natural energy flows that nourish, soothe, and calm the spirit. Beauty abounds in the uncontrolled, allowing surrendering flows. The changing seasons, the grace of falling leaves in autumn, a transition into the beauty of rebirth come spring.

Why do we resist by trying to control the circumstances and situations that come before us each day, and sometimes each hour of the day? We are in our heads when we do this. Intense thoughts and emotions circle again and again as we tense up and constrict, trying to figure out how to stop the outcome of a situation by manipulating and dominating it. Surrendering is not trying to control anything or anyone. It is a calm, inner peace that involves your whole being. Surrendering means we can trust enough to stop pushing, controlling, and forcing an issue to work out in our favor.

You have already had a taste of surrendering through the practices here, the feeling of freedom from unwanted thoughts through an allowing observation of them. As you move more and more into a surrendered state, you open up as a peaceful observer of life's natural flow, where you, as the observer, become one with an energetic flow that has powerful forces and endless possibilities within. Fortunately, as you match and align with the higher energy of surrender, you will attract better and better situations into your life, making life easier.

Through the experience of more ease and less struggle, you will
gain trust as you leave behind the old way of trying to control
everything through frustration and effort. A surrendered state
is saying yes to life and appreciating it. Once we say no and
resist life, we are reverting back to the false small mind, the
mind of problems and struggle.

HOW CAN YOU ACCEPT *EVERYTHING?*

The word surrender in most of the western world is thought
of as weakness rather than strength. We often picture a white
flag being waved in surrender by the one who loses, meaning
the one who surrenders is the "loser," and someone else is the
winner.

However, to be surrendered in Consciousness is a high,
energetic state. You may think it is difficult to consistently live
in a surrendered state, but what could be more difficult than
struggle and strife when things go "wrong"? To allow things to
be just as they are as we surrender into our breath and inner
Self may seem too easy. It may seem easier to continue doing
what feels normal, a consistent fight to make each situation
unfold "our way," resisting and being in opposition to what is
happening in the moment, refusing to "let it be," and living in
a state of anger and fear as a result.

Paradoxically, we become free when we surrender. We become
the captain of our lives, no longer reacting to what happened

or what someone said. There is much power in surrendering. We are transformed from the inside out because the reactionary false mind is no longer in evidence. With the false mind gone, we are free from the useless thoughts, emotions, and feelings that block and hinder life. That is true power.

Why not accept life however it presents itself? You will find that the more you surrender, the more life's flow becomes easier, and life becomes more manageable, gentler. You no longer fight or struggle. You are simply in your centered Self— in the heart of yourself—open and in full acceptance of what occurs in each slice of the present moment. There is much simplicity and power in surrender.

As you surrender moment to moment, you dissolve emotional pain from the past for good. Surrendering will also dissolve for good your worry about what the future may hold. Ease and joy can now be felt, rather than emotional pain. And it can be done as you breathe deeply in a calm and peaceful surrender, easily dissolving the weak lower energies of worry, anger, tension, and sadness—any low energy—and revealing the qualities of your innermost self, your True Self.

WHAT IS MEANT BY "YOUR TRUE SELF"?

You have had glimpses of your True Self many times. When you have been immersed, focused, and engaged in something you are enjoying, such as cooking, reading, or conversing. When you have been immersed and totally focused on a beautiful natural landscape that rendered you speechless. At times like these, you are accepting, aware, and allowing, and, as a result, appreciating life. You have found, in that moment, a state of surrendered inner peace and joy. Notice that meaningless and useless feelings and emotions of past pain or future worry that bring you down are not in evidence in moments like these. This is you at your best. This is you in your highest vibrational energy, attracting the same high-vibrational energy that will unfold as events and situations that will seem to just happen to you.

Don't be hard on yourself when you experience bouts of depressive, unwanted thoughts leading to feelings and emotions you do not want. We, humans, are surrounded by negativity daily. These negative "vibes" hinder and block a harmonious surrender to life. We feel lost amid the chaos that weighs us down.

Anger, fear, stress, guilt, resentment—any emotional pain—can become entangled, making us feel imprisoned and unable to find peace. This low energy produces weakness and a loss of vitality for life, causing over time a health complication through dis-ease. It is crucial to remember that the thoughts that give us emotional pain have no value whatsoever. They deflate our vitality and have the potential to shorten our lives. You must remember these inconsequential and meaningless thoughts *have no power at all!*

You do not need to feel the emotional pain of lower energy. By giving these lower-energy thoughts and emotions attention, you give them power. It is not easy to come between intense thoughts and the intense emotion that follows. However, you can, at the moment you recognize that an intense thought is coming through your space, relax your physical body through your breath, and your mind will follow suit.

You will, at times, be challenged to be your True Self in a surrendered state. At times, you may picture worst-case scenarios as unrelenting thoughts tormenting you with the emotional pain of anger and fearful worry.

Imagine a father's experience of tremendous anger and fear waiting for a teenage son whose arrival is long overdue. Thoughts of anger keep circling through the father's mind: "He knows how much I worry; why doesn't he answer my calls! He'll be punished for this. I won't agree to lend him the car anymore!" He paces back and forth, and as he stops to look out the window, he notices it's now dark, windy, and raining, adding fear to his anger.

HOW CAN WE SURRENDER TO A SITUATION WHEN WE ARE UPSET?

To regain the balance and harmony of his True Self, the father can calm himself through his breath. As the body relaxes, the mind will follow. Putting attention and awareness on the heart of your Self—your breath—is always a sure way to slow down a noisy mind.

The following practice, taking just seconds, will help you realize that anything that makes you feel bad—a thought, an emotion, a feeling, a memory, or any belief you want to let go of—is small, meaningless, and unimportant in comparison to the light of our surrendered True Self.

Practice: Dissolving weak lower energies as your True Self

As you go about your day and are burdened with unwanted thoughts that produce intense, burdensome emotions, do the following practice. Watch as harmful, useless energy dissolves into light:

1. Put aware attention on your breath as you inhale to calm yourself. A slow, deep inhale will help you exhale out all intense anxiety, tension, and fear. Inhale and exhale in the same way three or four times until you feel calm. Affirm, "Lower energy thoughts and feelings have no power over my innermost True Self."

2. Imagine a sun rising from the center of yourself. Imagine its brilliance increasing and becoming larger and larger, spreading out farther and farther, easily covering, with its powerful light, all the dark, weak energies that are useless

and do not make you feel good. Stay here as long as you like, imagining the brilliance easily covering the darkness.

3. Once you have released what doesn't make you feel good, revel in the freedom, the peace, and tranquility that the light of your True Self has created.

4. The bright light now brings clarity of thought and new insight and ideas about what to do about a situation. Ideas and insights may not be immediate; however, as you gain clarity, they will come more easily.

Remember that light easily blankets the darkness. There is never a struggle. In the same way, your innermost being, the light of your True Self, can easily dissolve the darkness of an intense thought. The more you surrender, the more relaxed and calm you become, imagining light dissolving all inner conflict, and the more you will gain from this practice.

The more the father in the example practices this process, imagining light easily overcoming darkness, the more he will release menacing thoughts, emotions, and feelings for good. Through a mind that is more spacious and clear, he will now receive inspirational ideas, revelations, and insights of a higher energy.

The truth of his fear of losing his son when he does not know his whereabouts can now be talked about in a peaceful, loving way. Feelings that reveal only truth now come to the surface. And he now has love and compassion in place of anger, and peace and calm in place of fear.

When his son arrives, the father expresses the truth of the situation. In calm clarity, he asks his son to help him come to an agreement of an appropriate time to come home and a responsible use of his phone to resolve the situation so he no longer worries when he lends him the car. His son is allowing for a calm solution because his father has come to the middle, where there is nothing to oppose. They have come to the midway point of understanding, where there is no duality, only harmony, and can come to an agreement more suitable and acceptable to both of them. As the father practices and aligns more and more with a peaceful, flowing surrendered state, his powerful True Self, his son can now respond in the same way.

As you go about your day, affirm your power often and sense your powerful light. Affirm, "Lower energy thoughts and feelings have no power at all." Then imagine a sunrise overpowering all darkness. In this way, you are easily dissolving all lower energies. You do not have to put forth effort or struggle, and as you let go, ease and calm empower you. Recognizing and realizing the truth of this affirmation will empower you. Little by little, you will no longer feel enslaved and overtaken by weak lower energies. It is important to begin affirming now so that at the moment of a crisis, you will realize the power of your True nature.

As you practice imagining the light of your True Self dissolving and vanishing lower energies, lower energies will surface less frequently and eventually cease altogether. You will now be living in a flowing, surrendered state.

You have now learned how to become *presence* through awareness of your life force energy within. And now you have learned how to dissolve meaningless lower energies through your powerful light so you can emerge as your True Self.

As you implement the practices in this book, you are now the power and force of pure Consciousness. You are not going against it; you are flowing with it.

A fulfilling life will be yours when, moment to moment, you are aware and surrendered inside an expanded place of higher energy, in celebration of a powerful, yet peaceful and harmonious You. You now understand that anything that makes you feel "bad" has no power over you. At that point, the possibilities for your life are vast and unlimited as you soar high, like a bird maneuvering life's flows and currents easily and effortlessly.

PRACTICES AND SUMMARY
OF CHAPTER TEN

SURRENDERING

The following practice is powerful, taking just seconds, dissolving through light all meaningless low energy that does not make you feel good and has no power at all.

1. Practice: Dissolving weak lower energies as your True Self

As you go about your day and are burdened with unwanted thoughts that produce intense, burdensome emotions, do the following practice. Experience harmful, useless energy dissolving:

a) Put aware attention on your breath as you inhale to calm yourself. A slow, deep inhale will help you exhale out all intense anxiety, tension, and fear. Inhale and exhale in the same way three or four times until you feel calm. Affirm, "Lower energy thoughts and feelings have no power over my innermost True Self."

b) Imagine a sun rising from the center of yourself, your innermost True Self. Imagine its brilliance increasing and becoming larger and larger, spreading out farther and farther, easily covering, with its powerful light, all the dark, weak energies that do not make you feel good. Stay as long as you like, imagining the brilliance easily covering the darkness.

c) Once what does not make you feel good is released, revel in the freedom, the peace, and tranquility that the light of your True Self has created.

The bright light now brings clarity of thought and new insight and ideas about what to do about a situation. Ideas and insights may not be immediate; however, as you gain clarity, they will come more easily.

2. Remember that the breath is the doorway to calm inner peace. As you physically calm down through your breath, the mind will follow.

3. Keep in mind that lower-energy thoughts, feelings, emotions, memories, and beliefs have no value. They are insignificant and inconsequential. You, as your True Self, are powerful, and more able than ever to create the life you want. When you feel burdened with unwanted thoughts and emotions, reconnect with your True Self. Affirm, "Lower

energy thoughts and feelings have no power at all." Imagine yourself like a brilliant sunrise easily overcoming all darkness.

SUMMARY

1. Surrendering is feeling inner peace from your head to your toes. As we follow surrendering's natural universal flow, we let go of all hardship, difficulty, and suffering.

2. As you surrender, you don't need to try to control anything or anyone. You do not need to struggle if something "did not turn out" the way you would have liked. Come back to your peaceful and flowing surrendered state through your breath.

3. In our culture, the word surrender is usually identified with weakness. The small false mind does not want to appear weak. This false mind resists because it thinks that to fight and "get its way" is power. Yet, paradoxically, we become free when we surrender. We no longer react to what someone says or does. We become the director of our life and no longer rely on an outside world for "happiness."

4. When we are in a surrendered flow, the defiant, small false mind is no longer fighting for our attention, demanding we feel the lower energies of anger, revenge, stress, and fear.

5. Aware and surrendered in pure Consciousness, like a bird, you can now maneuver a natural cosmic flow, its waves, and its currents, easily and effortlessly.

WHAT'S NEXT?

L ife can be challenging. However, it is only challenging because our world is dualistic, rarely coming to the center, where there is cooperation, not confrontation. The world that is so much a part of our daily lives seems only to exist on the fringes of drama and bad news.

Life is also only challenging because we allow exposure to and do not protect ourselves from the onslaught of bad news and drama.

You do not have to live on the periphery of limits and borders.

For the immeasurable depth of your heart dwells in your centered, truest Self in this very moment. By simply putting aware attention on your breath, you will let go of drama and bad news, leaving behind a world in serious jeopardy. And it can happen now, in this instant. You are being reminded here that it is really that easy!

However, we are tightly gripped by a world that tells us it's okay to feel anger and pain and fear.

Understand that when you feel weighed down and defeated, it comes from a mind that is in sync with the worldly mind that produces war, poverty, disparity, deception, and all suffering. It is one and the same.

Dwell, instead, in that rich space within, that you can easily access through the doorway of your breath.

You have now been opened and become receptive to a new way of being. Actually, a being that is truly you. How do you feel in each moment? If you feel down it is because you have taken in the turbulence and pollution of an outside world. Come back to your vantage point, your point of power, and simply observe the world.

Absorb the practices here by shining your powerful light on unwanted thoughts and emotions, taking just seconds to release.

Purposefully practice to be more positive, and your precious brain will thank you by re-wiring itself to help you be more positive in the future. Affirm your powerful truth often. Be present because the moment you become *presence*, you let go of all inner conflict.

FEEL THE CONNECTION
YOU HAVE WITH NATURE

Be engaged with the lull of lapping water, the melody of singing birds, and the flapping wings of butterflies and hummingbirds. You are a mirror to nature's limitless bounty and vibrant aliveness.

Nature sustains and nourishes our spirit. In its beauty, its stillness, and its soothing sounds we find our innermost self, our true nature and True Self. We find in nature the peace, calm, and joy that's always been there, yet, we've been looking for it all along. We are truly *that* and much more beneath the layers of sadness and defeat that we *believe* is who we are.

Stay in your timeless, peaceful and serene center where it is possible to live heaven on earth without crossing the fine line that can mean the destructive undoing of life.

That is how crucial it is to anchor the mind in positivity, in restful non-thought, in curiosity and awe.

Look up at a star-studded night sky and marvel. It contains the same Creative Intelligence that is the intricacy of your physical self, and that sparks the undeniable cosmic connection to your being.

Once we come into being, having realized who we really are, we can live it day by day, moment to moment. But it takes practice.

Ultimately, life is a game we must get good at and love to play. It is *the most* important game we've ever learned to play in our lives!

For when we live as our innermost, truest Selves, life becomes mystifyingly miraculous. We can now transform, evolve, and heal all life, including our planet. I will leave you with that!

CAN YOU HELP?

Please take a moment to leave a helpful review on
Amazon. I read all reviews and would greatly appreciate
yours. You would be helping to reach thousands around the
globe to live a better, more joyous life, free of inner turmoil.

With your helpful review, you would be
taking part in the urgent need for the evolution of
human Consciousness for a better world.

Thank you!

Darla Luz

ABOUT THE AUTHOR

Darla Luz is an award-winning writer who is passionate about expanding and evolving Consciousness throughout the world by writing about it in an easy to understand way. She lives what she has written in this book, knowing that our outer world always reflects the pure positivity of our inner world. Most days are spent doing her life's work of practicing her own expansion of Consciousness, and researching and writing about it so that she can help others be consciously aware in presence, free of struggle and inner turmoil. She enjoys taking nature walks with her family observing the natural wilderness along the riverbanks and lakesides near her home.

ACKNOWLEDGEMENTS

To my husband, Danny, for all the loving and patient support. Thank you for your light-hearted love of life! I couldn't have done it without you!

To my son, Brian, who was my first very professional editor. Thank you for reading every word of the manuscript and softening the blows of editing by always ending a critique with "what do you think?" Thank you to my daughter, Danielle, who added her own very professional and sound advice. My heart-felt thank you for all the joy you've brought into my life as babies, children, and now, loving and wise adults.

To my granddaughter, Vanessa, and to Samantha, the mother of three of my grandchildren, for their very important suggestions.

To my grandchildren, Christina, Vanessa, Alfonso, Mahal, and my youngest grandson, Ricky, who asked, "Are you dedicating the book to me, Grandma?" You, my children and grandchildren, are all shining stars who sing, perform, and create music, adding much light and joy to the world.

171

To my brother, Vince, and to my parents Vincent and Elvia in spirit, for being a part of my life.

To all at SPS Publishing, and especially to Gary Williams, author, for the help and encouragement to put my message out into the world. Also, thank you to my editor of the final draft, Katie Chambers, Beacon point LLC, for making the cutting process painless. And to my proof reader, Danielle Decker, for her helpful contribution.

I want to give my heart-felt appreciation to Sanaya Roman and Duane Packer @orindaben.com for their help in opening me to consciousness and its powerful life force that helped to realize this book.

And finally, to all friends and extended family members, including those who blur the word in-law, thank you for the pleasurable moments. To you, I also offer the light of joyous inner peace within these pages.